What's Happened to POLITICS?

Bob Rae

PUBLISHED BY SIMON & SCHUSTER CANADA
New York   London   Toronto   Sydney   New Delhi

Simon & Schuster Canada
A Division of Simon & Schuster, Inc.
166 King Street East, Suite 300
Toronto, Ontario M5A 1J3

This Simon & Schuster Canada edition August 2015

SIMON & SCHUSTER CANADA and colophon are registered
trademarks of Simon & Schuster, Inc.

Library and Archives Canada Cataloguing in Publication
Rae, Bob, 1948–, author
What's happened to politics? / Bob Rae.
Issued in print and electronic formats.
ISBN 978-1-5011-0341-4 (bound). — ISBN 978-1-5011-1805-0 (ebook)
1. Canada—Politics and government—21st century. I. Title.

JL65.R34 2015   320.971   C2015-903842-1
                                    C2015-903843-X

For information about special discounts for bulk purchases,
please contact Simon & Schuster Special Sales at 1-800-268-3216
or CustomerService@simonandschuster.ca.

Manufactured in the United States of America

10 9 8 7 6 5 4 3

ISBN 978-1-5011-0341-4
ISBN 978-1-5011-1805-0 (ebook)

For my parents, Saul and Lois, in loving memory.

Contents

Preface   ix

1 – What's Happened to Politics?   1

2 – What's Happened to Leadership?   23

3 – What's Happened to Policy?   49

4 – What's Happened to Aboriginal Peoples in Canada?   75

5 – What's Happened to Democracy in Canada?   95

6 – What's Happened to Canada in the World?   117

Conclusion   135

Further Reading   141

Acknowledgments   145

Index   149

Preface

Politics is, above all else, a public pursuit. Its concerns and goals are not ends in themselves. They are important only if they help us to answer one question: How do we make individual Canadians' lives better? There is an increasing sense that this has been lost in today's world, and we urgently need to change that. But how do we do it? What exactly is needed? And, most important, what are the consequences if we continue unchanged along the current course? Leaving partisan politics—for the second time—I have found myself reflecting on these questions, trying to make some sense of my life in public service. In doing so, I've come to realize that many of the values lacking in today's political landscape have their roots in the lessons I learned from my parents.

It has also been a year of reflection for very personal reasons:

2014 was the hundredth anniversary of the birth of both my parents. Though my father, Saul, had died some years before, my mother, Lois, spent her remarkable hundredth year enjoying her time among friends and family. Many years ago, one of my daughters came back from a visit to her grandmother and pronounced, "Dad! Granny knows everything!" Lois was indeed a wise and wonderful woman, and she spent most of her centennial year reminiscing about times past. During that year, I often visited her in the sitting room in my sister Jennifer's house, overlooking a park in Cabbagetown in Toronto. As we chatted, our conversation would inevitably turn to events in Canada and the world, and her words gave new perspective to my thoughts.

As summer turned to fall, though, her health began to fail. She had survived many ups and downs in the preceding years, and we all assumed she would bounce back again. But it was not to be, as her heart gave way and she drifted into longer and longer sleeps. Lois died two days after her one-hundredth birthday, surrounded by her children and much love.

My father, Saul, died in the winter of 1999, and I had long thought of writing a short book about his remarkable life and career. My mother had encouraged me in this idea, as she did in so many other things. But as I considered my parents' lives in the context of today's world, it dawned on me that there was more to their stories than biography. The more I examined the current state of politics and government in Canada, the more I saw in my parents the qualities that are so desperately needed today—passion for service, integrity, and patience.

I learned much about the art and science of politics from my father. Saul Rae was born in Hamilton, Ontario, in 1914 to immigrant parents. His father was a cutter in the clothing business and his mother ran a family vaudeville act, The Three Little Raes of Sunshine. He enrolled with an all-important bursary at University College, Toronto, in the fall of 1932 and began his studies in sociology. This was a relatively new discipline in those years, but it drew him in because of his deep interest in people. Saul Rae was a convivial man with a truly remarkable sense of humour and fun. He was also inquisitive and bright, and so was immediately attracted to the broad study of people and the societies they built.

Winning a Massey Fellowship upon graduation allowed Saul to travel to England to continue his studies, and he chose the London School of Economics, which had been founded by those earnest Fabians, Sidney and Beatrice Webb, forty years before. He quickly turned his attention to the new field of public opinion—it seemed ideally suited to his interest in people, what they thought, what made them tick. He studied with giants like Morris Ginsberg, a brilliant British sociologist, and Bronislaw Malinowski, one of the foremost twentieth-century anthropologists, and he attended Harold Laski's lectures on political theory. His doctoral thesis was titled "The Concept of Public Opinion and Its Measurement."

Saul later worked with George Gallup, the American pioneer of survey sampling techniques, and together they wrote *The Pulse of Democracy,* an early book about polling. My father then came back to Canada with his English-born wife, Lois, and joined the Canadian foreign service in 1940, where he spent his professional life until his retirement forty years later.

A decade after my father retired I became premier of Ontario, which was a turning point in my personal and political life. For the twenty years prior to that, I had seen myself as a man in opposition, fighting the good fight but never really expecting to be in power. Governing was the decisive political experience of my life. Choices were no longer about good and bad but often about awful and less awful. And every choice had ramifications, so thinking consequentially became vital.

Impulsive chess players might achieve a temporary advantage, but they rarely win games. So too in tennis, a game I learned from my dad from the age of five. My brother John once opined that if you want to win a game—and politics is a game, albeit one of the utmost importance, with far-reaching consequences—it's always a good idea to play against people who are worse than you are. That way you're more likely to succeed. As the architect of Jean Chrétien's three majority-winning election campaigns, he should know. But having the playing field tilted to your advantage isn't always possible. And if one is to succeed in politics—as in any game—certain things have to be remembered.

Control the centre, for the game is won by the side that successfully does so. In politics, some people complain that the centre is too crowded. That's nonsensical, because that's where most people are, and so that's where you have to be.

Every political leader has unique strong points that define him, but his overall success relies on having developed a better defence and countering any weak points to his skill set. Relying on his natural strengths will never be enough.

Patience and persistence count for a lot, and action is always more powerful than reaction. You can only create opportunities if you are the one in control of a situation.

Momentum is important, but it's critical to remember that

the same momentum that appears to be in your favour can turn on a dime. What makes a truly great politician is the ability to pivot, to improvise. The most important moments in a campaign occur when you're on your own with nothing to trust but your own instincts. If your instincts aren't well honed, you'll probably lose. But if you don't rely on them to respond to what your opponent is doing, you'll lose anyway, because simply going through the motions won't cut it.

Finally, as essential as natural talents or strategy might be, character is all-important; it's what allows you to deal with the setbacks that are unavoidable in life. What sets a true leader and competitor apart is her ability to stay focused on her goals, hold her temper, and keep any negative thoughts at bay. While the worst wounds are often self-inflicted, successful individuals know how to keep their mistakes to a minimum and are gifted with the ability to bounce back from any errors they do make. Attitude and character really do matter, and resilience is an important key to success.

This book is not a memoir or an exercise in nostalgia. It is not a tell-all or a morality play in which the hero inevitably wins out in the end. It is a reflection on some lessons learned, many after defeats rather than victories. It is a plea for political literacy and understanding, for citizens to look behind and beyond the partisan rhetoric and the spin. More than anything, it is meant to open a conversation, one that, as a country, we desperately need to have. There are certain questions that all Canadians should be asking themselves, their elected representatives, and their leaders. The time for that dialogue is now, and the need for it has never been greater. Let this serve as a way in.

What's Happened to
POLITICS?

CHAPTER ONE

WHAT'S HAPPENED TO POLITICS?

What exactly has gone wrong with politics? We need to be precise about the diagnosis before we can identify the remedies. That there is a widespread disillusionment with politics is undoubtedly true. There is a universal tendency to hearken back to a golden age of politics and public policy, to see through a gauzy lens to some time when men and women deliberated solemnly on the issues of the day, unsullied by the lure of lobbyists or the odour of self-interest. Such a time never existed. Politics has never been that way. No time has been free from the golden age of bullshit and the inevitable push and pull of who gets what, when, where, and how. But something has happened in our current time to create an aura of phony salesmanship that is even more pungent than the whiff of other times. What is it exactly?

I am not a social scientist, a philosopher, or a seer, but rather a mere mortal who has spent most of his life in politics, public service, the law, and education. I see no contradiction between a life of action and one of reflection, and I have tried to remain curious about the human condition. I do not see politics as inherently corrupt or evil—in fact, quite the opposite. I see it as a necessary endeavour, the deterioration of which troubles me not just because I do not like to see an important part of my life reviled, but because an improvement in the quality of public discourse is a good thing in itself. We are all somehow cheapened when politics and public life go sour.

The challenges we face are not just political. They involve broader issues in our society. Nor are the challenges confined to Canada. In fact, we can't understand them unless we realize that they have a lot to do with how the world is changing. The solutions do not lie just in our own country, then, nor are they entirely in our own hands. And that's where frustration, a sense of powerlessness, sets in.

It has much to do with what is happening to Canada and many other countries both economically and culturally. The most positive underlying force in any society is trust, something that is born of common understandings about how things will work out and how people will behave and treat one another. But as one of my colleagues observed during a cabinet meeting in Ontario two decades ago, "The water buffalo look at each other very differently when there's no water." When the bonds of trust among citizens are weakened, anything can happen, and this is part of what is at work today in societies both rich and poor. If inequalities are created that have no basis in values or understandings that are widely and deeply shared, resentment replaces trust as the operating force. That resentment grows and feeds on itself. Our politicians and political establishment must uphold and protect the people and institutions so integral to this trust, or they risk losing it permanently.

Before exploring the role of widening economic inequalities in eroding trust, let's start by putting some things in perspective. Canadians are lucky people—our collective standard of living is high, the country is beautiful, life is not terrible for most of us. We are a peaceable kingdom, people feel generally secure, and when questioned about how they're feeling, most Canadians express satisfaction with their lives and their prospects. We are not in the middle of a deep economic depression, though there are problems in some parts of the country. And yet something is missing; something nags at us saying things could be better.

At the end of the Second World War seventy years ago, Canadians were finally experiencing full employment, and with the return of peace came a period of sustained growth that was marked by a steady increase in the standard of living of average families. The provinces came into their own as education surpassed transportation as the key area of social investment. Quebec had its Quiet Revolution, and this had its parallels in every part of the country, with the evolution of social programs like the Canada Pension Plan, the introduction of universal health care, and the extension of the role of provinces and cities. It was a hopeful time for Canadians. They saw a great future for their children. They had faith in their leaders.

In 1967, Canada celebrated its centennial year by welcoming

the world to Montreal at an exposition that showed what an innovative and remarkable country we were. Few of us who remember that experience will forget it—the sense of pride and excitement we felt was tangible.

Ironically, what we didn't realize at the time was that this was in fact a turning point. It all came down to money. Though our federal government had a balanced budget in 1969, it would not see another one until 1998. Both government spending and taxes increased, but unemployment edged up higher through the 1970s and 1980s. By 1990, with the rise in interest rates and the adjustments brought about by the free trade agreement with the United States, Canada's largest province, Ontario, faced its most severe economic crunch since the Great Depression.

The challenges of those years really forced Canadians across the political spectrum to come to terms with what had been a national problem twenty-five years in the making. From the early 1970s onwards, all governments, of all stripes, had increased taxes and by and large got away with it because steady inflation concealed the increases. Simply put, when you got a wage increase on January 1, it would hide the underlying tax increase. This changed when high interest rates and a collapsed economy drove inflation out.

When tax increases resulted in lower paycheques, the understandable reaction soon followed. I can well remember a meeting in an auto workers hall in 1991 when I was told, "I voted to tax the rich, but I didn't think you meant me." As a skilled worker in an auto plant, the speaker would have been making a good income, but that didn't produce a strong desire to share it with the government.

The healthier growth that re-emerged in the mid-1990s was good news, as was the decision to use that growth and higher revenues to get budgets back into balance and even pay off some debt with the surpluses that followed. Things were going so well that some commentators even gloated that the business cycle and economic crises were a thing of the past. But several mini jolts (like the collapse of the dot-com bubble in 2000) and one big mess (the implosion of Wall Street and the financial crisis of 2008 and onwards) should surely have disabused anyone of this idea. Since then, the world economy has returned to a semblance of order, but the underlying unease Canadians still feel should remind us all of two things—the fragility of recoveries and the interconnectedness of the world economy. Look at how Alberta's economy suddenly shifted from one that outperformed much of the world to one that is struggling with the impact of drastically lower resource prices. The people in Canada's most oil-rich province now have to adapt to the realities of a global economy that is affected by a number of forces outside of their control. And the political changes we have seen in the last few months are a reflection of those underlying challenges.

The moral origin of the financial crisis of 2008 was, undoubtedly, a greed that knew no limits. Dodgy mortgages bled their way into the world financial system and blew any sense of stability to smithereens. There was no secure ground anywhere, and the crisis flew from the financial sector to all others and from one country to the next. Those countries with more stable banking systems and healthier public account balances held on better than others, but no one was exempt from the impact, and no one would be immune from another outbreak.

Following the financial crisis, personal, corporate, and government debts shot back up after declining for fifteen years, and they are now at a point where another blow similar to the one we experienced in 2008–09 would be, quite simply, devastating.

Underpinning all of this upheaval is the age-old question, "How do these changes affect the condition of the people?" The turmoil of the last two decades has revealed the extent to which the forces we sum up in the easy word "globalization" have in fact benefitted those who already control the wealth, the now infamous 1 percent, just as the kleptocracy in Russia and the elite in China have skimmed the cream off the extraordinary riches to be had when a state-owned and -controlled economy suddenly does a 180-degree turn and sells off assets to the bidders with the best connections. Even when some economists tell us that things are going well, with lower unemployment and taxes under control, the general population is not comforted. There is a new label for those whose lives go from paycheque to paycheque—"precarious workers." The answers and explanations that supposed experts and leaders provide are inconsistent and insufficient. No wonder Canadians feel distrustful and alarmed. No wonder they feel powerless.

———

Given this unstable economic landscape and the need to reaffirm our social bonds, one would think that there is both an opportunity and a need for politicians to more readily engage a citizenry that is better informed and more accessible than ever before. There is a chance to move past the slogans and

the election speeches to engage in meaningful and lasting discourse, dialogue, and debate. But instead, we are greeted with
just the opposite. Anyone watching politics in North America
and around the world knows that today, parties are instead focused on running permanent campaigns. Politics has become a
full-time business in which incessant campaigning trumps real
governance.

The speed at which politics takes place is only multiplied
by the impact of digital communication and social media. This
is widely recognized, and it is not entirely novel—even going
back to the French Revolution, one finds popular songs, car-
toons, and flyers that proclaimed Marie Antoinette's alleged excesses both sexual and personal. But in today's world, with the
Twittersphere and the Internet dispensing information more
broadly, the lid of respectability is off. Gossip and rumour are
grist to the mill, patience is a vice, and while the laws of libel
are there for a few hardy (and well-off) souls, they hardly act
as much prevention. As a result, the level of public discourse
has fallen off badly.

A recent book by Sasha Issenberg, *The Victory Lab*, brilliantly describes how big data has been mobilized in an attempt
to ensure political success, accurately making the point that a
good part of what is going on in these permanent campaigns is
an exercise in "creating the electorate." The question of who
votes is as important as how they vote. President Obama's
success in 2008 was all about creating a bigger, younger electorate, because Democrats knew that if they could succeed in
doing this, they would be far more likely to win. The Obama
campaign successfully employed a combination of volunteer
recruitment and enthusiasm, and it paid enormous attention

to analytics and systems. It was also an effort bankrolled by unprecedented fund-raising. The 2010 midterm election, however, was a setback for Obama, largely because a discouraged and disheartened electorate stayed away from the polls. In the campaign for the second term, the Obama team realized that unless they grew the electorate back, they would lose the election. Sasha Issenberg describes in detail the analytical effort, and the money, involved in helping to achieve that goal. Savour the language of the new politics from this revealing book:

> A July EIP [experiment-informed program] designed to test Obama's messages aimed particularly at women found that those between 20 and 40 support scores showed the greatest response to his arguments about women's health and equal-pay measures. Their low support index meant that other indicators of their partisanship pointed strongly to likely Republican attitudes: here was one thing (probably the only thing) that could pull them to Obama. As a result, when Obama unveiled a track of his direct-mail program addressing only women's issues, it wasn't to shore up interest among core parts of the Democratic coalition, but to reach over for conservatives who were uniquely cross-pressured on gender concerns.

Today, the electorate is sliced, diced, dissected, and divided to an extent unimaginable even fifteen years ago. All parties are segmenting the electorate and are adopting the tactics of companies selling a packaged product. Consultants share the same enthusiasm for branding a leader or a party as they do for a bar of soap. Occasionally a leader or issue will mobilize the public, but when confronted with the challenge of governing (as President Obama certainly was by the financial crisis he had to meet head-on), often his actions are not able to match the eloquence of his words. Obama had to make difficult choices, and the right-wing media onslaught did not let up for a single minute. Voters started to see him as indecisive. The trouble with pursuing politics as a business is that it has helped to create a cynical, fractured electorate that doesn't know whom to trust or what to do.

Compounding this is the way in which messaging has become narrow and repetitive, with every activity of the candidate a rote repeat of prepackaged, whitewashed slogans. Defining the opposition in as vicious and dogmatic a way as possible is now more than half the game. The other half is repeat, repeat, repeat the message that has been crafted as your brand. In Parliament, Question Period is now a cycle of sound bites that have usually been written by someone else. Televised debates are rarely real exchanges but rather ships firing volleys at one another amid efforts to get the message out. Meaningful questions are replaced with cynical lectures and prescribed messaging. And until the right questions are posed, satisfactory answers will be in short supply. No wonder Canadians are disenchanted with what they perceive as manufactured debate and stage-managed performances in the House.

The trouble with pursuing politics as a business is that it has helped to create a cynical, fractured electorate that doesn't know whom to trust or what to do.

The full title of Sasha Issenberg's book is *The Victory Lab: The Secret Science of Winning Campaigns,* and therein lies a premise that is problematic. What is missing is that leadership and political engagement are as much an art as a science. They have to do with good organization as much as inspiring serious efforts that bring about change. Pollsters and campaign advisors are in the business of making money, and part of the way they sell their wares is by telling us that they are wizards, that they have access to a secret science. There is no magic, no black box, and no secret science, but the more we think there is, the more we give up our rights and responsibilities to demand more from the political process.

———

Young voters, in particular, should be the ones shouting loudest for political institutions and representatives that genuinely reflect what they want and need. The steep decline in election participation among younger voters points to a gnawing distrust and disaffection, which will tend to spread more widely as the habits learned at an early age persist through time. If there is no positive memory of the first time voting or becoming politically active in some way, the apathy can only spread.

There is a lot of evidence to suggest that driving turnout down, "depressing the vote," is just what conservative parties want. An older, richer demographic votes; a poorer, younger electorate does not. A couple of solutions have been bandied about: compulsory voting and easier voting. Compulsory voting would have a hard time taking hold in any country with a rights-based written constitution. It's hard to see how the freely made decision not to vote could be made subject to a penalty. The Australian example is not really relevant—that decision to levy fines on people for staying home was made some time ago, and in a very different political culture.

A combination of lowering the voting age and making it much easier to vote might have more impact on turnout. Part of the answer might be to lower the voting age to sixteen and start basic civic education in primary school. Allowing people to vote at home digitally would make sense as well. It is hard to see how a population that can do its banking on a cell phone should be told that it is too complicated and insecure to vote in the same way.

It is hard to see how a population that can do its banking on a cell phone should be told that it is too complicated and insecure to vote in the same way.

There is a deeper reason for the disengagement of younger voters, and that is the overhang of the baby boom generation and the issues that preoccupy this very powerful group of voters. If hospital waiting lists and pensions, to give just two examples, are issues dominating the landscape, and problems affecting younger people, such as education costs, housing, and help to families, are given short shrift, it should come as no surprise that these same under-thirties ask themselves, "What's in it for me?" In turn, the dismal turnout rates of precarious voters in marginal jobs makes parties feel even more strongly that there's little point in appealing to those who have turned off.

As more and more voters turn away from the election

process, it is worth considering how politicians reach out to this increasingly distant electorate, namely through polls. Pollsters today speak with nostalgia about a time when the response rate to their questions was well above 80 percent. In the 1930s and 1940s, the Gallup organization did door-to-door surveys, and in time, as landline phones became universal, moved to phone surveys that were more or less reliable. Those days are gone, and as a result the polling business itself is in something of a crisis.

It would be an exaggeration to say that polling today is in completely speculative territory. But the inability to get reliable answers to questions should surely make us pause. Not that the pollsters themselves will admit that anything is really wrong. The political parties, who poll regularly and who thereby claim more vocally that they know where they stand in relation to popular opinion, are in constant contact with the public and with their supporters, raising money and waging propaganda campaigns in yet another aspect of the permanent campaign.

But the published polls are often all over the map, and pollsters rarely say what their response rate is, let alone clearly indicate their techniques in response to the disappearing voices at the end of the line. Some use the Internet as a way of connecting, others establish panels in an effort to achieve a representative sample, and still others insist that by adding cell phones and a larger sample they are able to assess opinion very well, thank you. It is a business as notorious as politics itself for backbiting and running down the opposition, as new entries into an already crowded field are derided for their techniques, their samples, their questions, and, above all, their reliability.

And just as the process of polling has changed, the political parties themselves have transformed the way they do business as they seek to mobilize their base and achieve success in response to what the polls tell them.

In the early 1960s, the New Democratic Party pioneered the door-to-door canvass, returning to the same home three or four times in order to identify a reliable pool of voters to be pulled on Election Day. For the NDP, identifying and pulling was essential, because as a third party it was harder for them to rely on a wave of general support to get people elected. Other parties with larger volunteer bases soon borrowed this technique.

Today, we live in a different world. Canadian pollsters are reluctant to admit that response rates on the phone are way down, that the landline is no longer universal, that people aren't at home, and that finding a reliable statistical base is in fact notoriously difficult and hard to measure. Experienced political canvassers in all parties will also tell you that volunteers are not as numerous, that people are either not at home or don't answer the door, and that it is more difficult to get the IDs that are the key to a successful Election Day organization. Parties no longer have the same direct response from or interaction with the voters they seek to reach. The result is a more impersonal approach that emphasizes the breadth of a party's reach over the depth of its conversation. The Conservatives' machine under the leadership of Stephen Harper relies heavily on robocalling and building a base of reliably identifiable supporters, and their strategy has now been imitated by the other parties.

A growing group of citizens—and a majority of those under thirty—don't vote, almost as a matter of principle. The number of "don't know, don't care" subscribers is on the rise, and the length of time that many are taking to come to judgment is growing as well. Political parties are trying to figure out how to mobilize and tap into these sentiments à la Obama and realizing how tough a challenge it really is given the lack of dependable information at their disposal.

———

At the same time that they try to connect with the broadest base of voters possible, political parties seek to refine their message into a digestible form that can be efficiently delivered and easily consumed. Like other governments before him, Mr. Harper's has made use of such government advertising to promote programs and ideas closely associated with his leadership. There has been a systematic effort to make the Conservative brand the Canada brand. Soon after being elected in 2006, the Conservatives insisted that all government announcements should refer not to the "government of Canada" but to "the Harper government." Wordsmithing and advertising have become centralized, closely linking parties' announcements to a reinforcement of their ideology. Ministerial speeches, answers in Question Period, running commentary on the political shows—the list goes on: every contact point with the public has been usurped as an opportunity to deliver the message of the day, week, month, or year. Nothing is left to chance, or indeed to spontaneity. The permanent campaign means repetitive and relentless bombardment. And if truth is the first casualty in war it certainly is in politics as well.

One writer in the last century more than any other understood the universe we are now living in. We even use his name to describe this universe—"Orwellian."

This is a world where things are not as they appear to be, where words are used to hide, twist, and pervert but never to describe, where propaganda triumphs and truth is left on the slaughterhouse floor. Orwell *And if truth is the first casualty in war it certainly is in politics as well.* loved language, and he understood more clearly than almost any of his contemporaries that the control of language, and of collective memory, is the key weapon of the totalitarian state.

In a talk at Carleton University given in 2013, the noted pollster, broadcaster, and writer Allan Gregg, much of whose professional life has been spent advising Conservative governments both federally and provincially, connected the dots between the universe Orwell was describing in *1984* and the state of current politics. The late Christopher Hitchens, coming from a different political perspective, wrote one of his last books on Orwell's legacy, pointing out with his usual panache that on the great issues of his time—and ours—Orwell was not only right but painfully accurate.

Orwell's word for the ruling method of analysis of Big Brother's regime was "doublethink"—"To know and not to know, to be conscious of complete truthfulness while telling carefully constructed lies." As both Gregg and Hitchens point out, there's a lot of doublethink going on out there, and it's more ideologically driven than we might realize.

Take something like the decision to end the long-form census in 2010. There was a time when the question of how to handle the census would have been a concern removed from politics. All parties and governments accepted the objectives of reliable data, minimizing intrusiveness and coercion, and ensuring privacy. Public servants rightly pride themselves on their objectivity. And so they should—they serve the people.

The issue at hand is not just about the long-form census. It's about the assault on Canada's best political traditions and an assault on reason itself. Once, in a debate on the criminal justice system and the growing evidence that putting more people behind bars was not going to be effective in deterring crime, a minister of justice famously said, "We don't need evidence, we know what's right and what's wrong."

There are two erroneous assumptions here: The first is the belief that the truth has nothing to do with science and reason but instead is simply a matter of faith. The second is that the way to get things done is to centralize power and then use that power to control the message, destroy the opposition, and achieve the desired legislative result.

This is an attack on common sense, but it is also more than that. It leads to a dangerous transformation in democratic and constitutional institutions themselves. It is important to rise above demonology and understand how we have reached this point and how deeply ingrained this dismissal of reason is in modern politics, elections, and the management of government. It will take a remarkably determined effort to change course, for the transformation is far more systemic than most Canadians now realize. A simple change in government will not be enough, because the parties that succeed will have learned to mimic at least some of their predecessor's style.

Lack of reliable engagement with the electorate and the flight of good judgment are of consequence not just for incumbents, challengers, and their handlers, but for voters as well. If the facts, opinions, and data to which politicians respond are spotty or unrepresentative, what can be done to ensure that voters' voices are heard and politicians' platforms are honest and clear? With an increased availability of information comes the responsibility to use it properly. Political parties must employ the right tools—targeted digital communication, efficient volunteer bodies, reliable data sourcing—to renew and refresh their engagement with people of all ages. Politicians must make a shift away from speaking *to* Canadians and instead look to once again speak *with* them.

———

The content of the exchange between citizens and their elected representatives is important in and of itself, but so too is the quality of that exchange. The methods we use to convince people can either cheapen or ennoble public life. In her remarkable novel on the exercise of power in the world of Henry VIII's court, *Bring Up the Bodies*, Hilary Mantel writes, "What is the nature of the border between truth and lies? It is permeable and blurred because it is planted thick with rumour, confabulation, misunderstandings and twisted tales. Truth can break the gates down, truth can howl in the street; unless truth is pleasing, personable and easy to like, she is condemned to stay whimpering at the back door."

A study of propaganda in the First World War was aptly called *The First Casualty*, referring to the idea that truth is the

first thing discarded by all sides as they attempt to move opinion in the name of a cause.

Just as that war unleashed an unprecedented level of death and violence, so too it involved the almost total mobilization of the public and the wholesale manipulation of the popular press to create negative stereotypes of the enemy and to drive public opinion into a frenzy of support for the war effort.

Each medium of communication in every era—newspapers, movies, radio, television, and now social media—has its own particular method of persuasion. And at every point, political propaganda has borrowed heavily from commercial techniques. Mass advertising dates back a couple of hundred years, but political campaigns and management have never been strangers to the world of money. They have always understood the power of an image.

The famous Sir John A. Macdonald telegram to the Canadian Pacific Railway—"Send another ten thousand"—was hardly the first act of corruption in the history of modern Canada, and it won't be the last. Macdonald was the inventor of the political picnic in Canada, massive events attended by thousands of people. He made unabashed use of his image as the Grand Old Man of the country to tug on the heartstrings of Canadians as he headed into his final campaign.

His approach resonated with his contemporaries. Like Macdonald, Sir Wilfrid Laurier was his own image maker. They were both actors, but their acting did not conceal their substance, it magnified it. They kept themselves aloof, a bit apart, but they were not sheltered by handlers to the point where they could not be reached by ordinary people. Their authenticity and the truth in their messages resonated all the more for that.

How different political life seems today. Political leaders are coiffed, dressed, managed, scripted, controlled, and presented to the public not so much as real people but as packaged products. The character and courage of the past is desperately needed today. We should not merely gaze wistfully at the best of our political ancestors, seeing them as anachronistic models of a lost era. Rather, we must hold them up as an example of the power to be found in genuine connection between citizen and public servant.

The media presenting the politicians are every bit as synthetic and packaged as the people and causes they are trying to analyze. Whether through newspapers, television, radio, blogs, Twitter, or Facebook, there is no room for accident or spontaneity, for market share is as fiercely contested as political support. And at the root of it is money—the money to be made by advertising, consulting, advising, and persuading. In Canada, we have managed to keep our politics a multimillion-dollar business, but in the United States it is a multibillion-dollar affair. The American Supreme Court has opined that political advertising is an extension of free speech, and so any efforts to limit spending and contributions have been largely unsuccessful. This American model of modern democracy is being spread by armies of consultants and advisors who now turn up on the doorsteps of countries throughout the world. *The Selling of the President* by Joe McGinniss, which described the American presidential campaign of 1968, now has its parallels in the selling of

Money, as much as principle, dictates whether you can run for high office.

whatever leader or party comes to mind. Money, as much as principle, dictates whether you can run for high office.

Money talks most, of course, in election time. When he was president of the National Citizens Coalition, Stephen Harper did his level best to challenge Canada's electoral laws, with their limits on party spending and advertising, and he did succeed in one respect. In the view of the Supreme Court of Canada, so-called third party spending could not be completely restricted because of the Charter's strictures on freedom of speech. But the central foundation of Canadian election law—that spending by parties both nationally and in each constituency should be limited—has stayed intact.

However, Canada's laws are silent about spending between elections, and so permanent fund-raising by Conservatives has led to devastatingly effective and ongoing negative advertising. They understood long before either the Liberals or the NDP the need to expand membership, connect members to the party by repeated requests for money and support related to particular issues, and use that money effectively every day, year in and year out. Gentlemanly knocks on the doors of the largest banks, companies, and unions just before election time are a thing of the past. Today, we have to live with a steady diet of attack ads day and night, long before an election campaign is officially launched.

Mr. Harper's second move was to turn off the support tap from the government for all political parties. When Jean Chrétien made his own changes to election funding laws just before his retirement, he limited the amounts individuals and others could give but allowed for public support of parties through subsidies based on vote totals for each party. Realizing his competitive advantage with a broader membership base and a new culture of fund-raising and giving, Mr. Harper tapered off the government subsidy, forcing the other parties to enter the brave new world of the permanent campaign.

All of this has distorted our perspective of the political process. Though much focus is given to the spending and running of campaigns, we should not be fooled by what has been aptly called "electoral symbolism" to conclude that voting and elections is all that democracy is about.

Politics is not just about who wins what election. The mobilization that occurs in elections for one party or candidate or another is only a small piece of the puzzle of understanding how the current political process impacts the individual citizen. What happens after and between elections tells us far more about democracy than voting, pure and simple.

Frequently, pundits will talk about "an emerging consensus" on a range of issues, which is then presented as an established fact. But this fails to explain how what was once a prevailing opinion can dramatically change and how the pushing and prodding of interest groups and powerful leadership that persists over time can in fact alter the framework of respectability. Ideas do not appear out of thin air, nor do the choices that are made about which agendas to put in front of a parliament or a city council. An analysis of power relations would tell us more than which lobbyists and interest groups seem to have the most influence on decision makers. It would go further and explain how some proposals never even get discussed, let alone modified, while others become the focus of controversy. On a televised debate, what is left unsaid can be just as important—sometimes more so—than what is discussed. Who sets the agenda, and on whose behalf, is as important an issue in politics as who votes and who stays home. That this reality is studied less than endless polling or the personalities of leaders is itself a commentary on where we are today.

When we ask ourselves what's happened to politics, it is important to remember how some issues come to the fore while others never make it to the table. In a time of economic, political, and social uncertainty, Canadians must ask themselves if the messages being marketed to them reflect what they need to know or just what their elected representatives are willing to tell them. Politics is not simply a game for politicians in which citizens observe from the sidelines. The waging of permanent campaigns, with their rote messaging and endless spending, means that we are all more impacted by and tied into the political process than ever before. But how do we observe and engage with what is an increasingly opaque institution? By looking past the packaging of their politicians to examine the content of the product, Canadians can stake a renewed claim in this changing political landscape and spur those who are supposed to work on their behalf from simply acting into something approaching authenticity.

Who sets the agenda, and on whose behalf, is as important an issue in politics as who votes and who stays home.

CHAPTER TWO

WHAT'S HAPPENED TO LEADERSHIP?

When I asked my dad why he left the world of polling as a young man of twenty-five, he said simply, "It was the war. There were more important things to worry about. Anyway, turning heads is more important than counting heads."

Wise words. And always a challenge, particularly in a time of cynicism.

Leadership can be defined as the ability to develop a vision, a plan of action, an approach to a problem or a situation; to persuade others to accept and embrace that vision, plan, or approach; and to take the steps that are necessary to make it happen.

The three components—vision, persuasion, implementation—are all required for effective leadership. Being weak in any one area will prevent success. Having a fuzzy vision will make it difficult to persuade and even harder to take action. Conversely, a vision that is so rigid it can't be affected by what is happening in the world will lead to catastrophic results if implemented. Edmund Burke once said memorably that "nothing is more dangerous than to govern in the name of a theory." His withering assault on the French Revolution starts from that single premise, that the idea of equality could become a tyranny because of its ruthless implementation. Leaders must see things as they are, and they must also be able to imagine how they should be.

But merely envisioning change does not bring it about. Effective leaders do not simply make a command and watch it happen. They cajole, compromise, demand, and negotiate as needed. Leadership is thus different from both prophecy and management. Garry Wills's brilliant little book on the subject of leadership, *Certain Trumpets: The Nature of Leadership*, begins with the simple premise that leaders need followers and that the criticism of leaders for moving too slowly is often misplaced because it puts too much value on the vision and too little on persuasion and getting it done. Purity is a necessary recipe for sainthood, but not all saints are good leaders (and not all good leaders are saints).

Leadership is not a voice crying in the wilderness, aloof and apart. It requires an ability to command as well as to inspire, to learn in the process of collaboration and to build a team with a common purpose that can take action and execute the change they envision. Great social and religious movements arise because of the confluence of events and leadership—events or conditions that cry out for change, and leaders who are able to express the pain of life as well as the dream of that change and a better world. But the transition from protest to power can be painful, and the leaders able to voice the need for change are not necessarily those who can actually get things done, with all the messy compromise that involves. Eloquence is not enough, because the walk is even more important than the talk.

Few people possess all three necessary qualities. Some may speak well while having nothing of substance to say. Others may have idealistic visions but can't execute them or convince others of their merit. Trying to lead effectively while lacking one or more of those vital components is bound to fail. The best leaders are well-rounded, able to draw on whatever skill suits the particular situation at hand. They are determined, insightful, shrewd, and, most important, able to command the attention of the people around them.

———

If turning heads is more important than counting them, and the way we try to turn heads matters even more, it follows that leadership matters. This is about more than the leaders of a particular moment; it requires some perspective on the kind of leadership Canadians should be looking for in general.

Henry Ford is reputed to have said that if he'd given people what they wanted, he'd have settled on faster horses. Feeding the current appetite is not a recipe for long-lasting change and innovation. Moods and desires change, and opinions and feelings shift when people are presented with different realities and facts. Harold Macmillan's famous answer to the question, "What happened to some of your plans when you first became prime minister?" was "Events, dear boy, events." The role of leadership is helping people to understand and interpret events as they come unexpectedly, and to make decisions that might at first seem implausible.

While we often think of leadership as a social or relational issue, it actually starts with the self. "Great people" biographies or memoirs are replete with stories of how character is formed at an early age and how identity itself starts with a healthy personality making its way in the world from dependency to walking on her own. Leadership combines the discipline to be alone with the ability to work in a collegial way. But a leader must first know his or her mind, character, and self.

> *All leadership is rooted in the culture and values of the place and time where it is being exercised, and it can only be fully understood in that context.*

All leadership is rooted in the culture and values of the place and time where it is being exercised, and it can only be fully understood in that context. A skilled and gifted leader will know how to communicate and persuade, what language to use, what symbols to refer to, how to connect with the group.

The contrasting challenges and responses of successful politicians over time tell us much about political leadership. They also help us to see our own leaders in the light of history and experience. James MacGregor Burns's fine biography of Franklin Roosevelt describes the former president as "the lion and the fox"—the lion because he gave people courage and hope in the midst of the Great Depression, and the fox because he was so deeply crafty in his methods. Roosevelt was vilified by the economic royalists of his day, but they did not grasp the deeply conservative nature of his goal. He did not want to eradicate capitalism, he wanted to save it from its worst excesses and restore confidence in a system that had collapsed in Europe, thereby producing the grotesque excesses of Hitler, Mussolini, and Stalin. There were many in the United States, like Louisiana governor Huey Long and the radio commentator Father Charles Coughlin, who preached the need for root and branch change and flailed away at what they saw as the corruption of the political game. Rather than react to such posturing or stubbornly hold to a single stance, Roosevelt proved ever pragmatic. He frustrated friend and foe alike by tacking left and right like a sailor in a deep storm, abandoning positions and advisors as it suited his larger purpose but always focusing on his vision of the broader need for reform.

Two British contemporaries of Roosevelt, Neville Chamberlain and Winston Churchill, provide a sharp contrast to Roosevelt's skill set as a leader. Chamberlain reflected the antipathy to another war that was deeply ingrained in the British public, and his complacent, cautious approach to management of the economy was matched by a determination to find some basis for peace with Hitler's dictatorship.

This policy of appeasement made Chamberlain popular. The nascent British Institute of Public Opinion tracked his rising popularity, which increased steadily as he courted Hitler and Mussolini and orchestrated the pact at Munich in September 1938, which bought a few months' peace in exchange for the dismemberment of a sovereign country, Czechoslovakia. Chamberlain was convinced he had brought "peace in our time." He calculated brilliantly what people wanted to hear, and he gave it to them. It is often forgotten today how popular Chamberlain was at the time. He had millions of willing accomplices.

Chamberlain's rival in the Conservative Party was Winston Churchill, who spent the entire decade of the 1930s out of favour and out of office. Churchill opposed any compromise with those like Gandhi who were seeking fundamental change in the British Empire. And, almost alone among the politicians of his day, he identified the uniquely poisonous nature of Hitler's leadership and the threat it posed to Germany, Europe, and the world. Robert Rhodes James, a Conservative historian, wrote a brilliant study called *Churchill: A Study in Failure*. It took stock of Churchill's life to the end of the 1930s and rightly concluded that, had he died at sixty-five, his career would have been seen as an eccentric, careening catastrophe. He thundered and railed against the orthodoxies of his day, an uncompromising voice in the wilderness. Chamberlain, by contrast, had approval ratings in the high 50s right up until the outbreak of war in September 1939, and it was only as events unfolded that his world, and his popularity, collapsed.

Leadership finds its deepest resonance when the vision and public opinion become one.

Churchill's star rose as surely as Chamberlain's fell. While Churchill's views on India and Gandhi remained reactionary and deeply racist, he grasped one hard truth—that the unremitting evil of Hitler and Nazism could only be stemmed through military resistance.

He was the lion that roared, the voice that defined the cause of freedom at the moment it was sorely needed. Leadership finds its deepest resonance when the vision and public opinion become one. These moments do not happen often, or easily, and they don't necessarily last very long, but in Churchill, the public heard what they needed to hear.

Roosevelt, by contrast, understood instinctively that his staying in power required a profound respect for the public mood. A Wilsonian Democrat in the First World War, Roosevelt saw his country turn inward after the battle to bring the United States into the League of Nations was lost. His struggle with polio in the 1920s forced him to watch and reflect on what it would take to regain power. Roosevelt was the master reader of men, of their ambitions and foibles. He knew moods could change, and he was not one to confront a wall of resistance. He wanted power, and he was prepared to compromise to get it and keep it.

This did not mean he lacked vision. Quite the contrary. On the two great issues of his time in the 1930s—economic recovery and dealing with the dictators of the day—he sensed what he had to do. He knew that his promise in 1932 to balance the budget would have to be jettisoned once the bottom fell out of the financial markets and depression was all around him.

Roosevelt's Fireside Chats were brilliant examples of using a popular medium of communication—in this case, radio—to bring people into his confidence, to let them know he understood their pain and wanted to do something about it. The radio was not used rhetorically to whip people up. The voice in the corner of the kitchen or the living room was not a loud voice, and Roosevelt did not harangue his listeners. He was trying to create a sense of security more than a sense of enthusiasm.

He was attempting to explain fairly complex issues without lecture or condescension, and people responded in kind. When Herbert Hoover was president, his correspondence was, on average, eight hundred letters per day. From his earliest time in office Roosevelt received roughly eight thousand letters a day. It was a dialogue, a conversation.

The same give-and-take took place in Roosevelt's inner circle. Those who were closest to Roosevelt in 1932 and who formed the key members of his Brains Trust—people such as Raymond Moley, Rexford Tugwell, and Adolf A. Berle, Jr.— quickly found themselves competing for the president's ear when bright newcomers appeared on the scene. Different aides were surprised to learn that the president had asked them independently to work on projects, often competing with one another. His work methods seemed chaotic, but there was method enough there: he wanted to hear from different perspectives, and, not having strong policy biases himself, he was, as mentioned, ruthless about jettisoning ideas and colleagues when it seemed necessary. Pragmatism trumped idealism.

Thus the New Deal, a series of domestic programs that profoundly altered America's political foundations, was progressive and conservative, radical and prudent, bold and cautious. Its one consistency was its determination to provide people with some hope, a hope based not on rhetoric but on real steps to get them back to work. But, to the frustration of Roosevelt's many critics on the left, there was no ideology and no orthodoxy to his method. Economist John Maynard Keynes, political theorist Harold Laski, and American Socialist leader Norman Thomas came away from their encounters with Roosevelt both charmed and frustrated. They enjoyed

FDR's banter and his curiosity. But they couldn't bring him around to a consistent way of thinking.

One of life's truly wise souls, Justice Oliver Wendell Holmes, who was reaching the end of his life just as the New Deal began, once said of Roosevelt's illustrious cousin Teddy: "Second rate intellect, first rate character." The same could well be said about Franklin. An insight so often overlooked by academic observers of politics is that braininess matters less than character. Roosevelt was an optimist, a charmer, a man who successfully feigned being an extrovert while remaining a mystery to his closest family and friends.

Leadership starts with the individual, but it avoids the sin of narcissism only if it is about more than the self. Roosevelt personified the needs and aspirations of a generation who were without work and without hope. When he died, a reporter spotted a man crying and asked him if he knew the president. "No," the man replied, "but he knew me." Roosevelt's abilities to see just what people needed, to persuade others to share in his vision, and, ultimately, to enact his plan—to be both the lion and the fox as the situation dictated—are what set him apart as a leader of the highest order. In today's era of economic uncertainty, Canadians must ask themselves whether they see the same courage and substance in the leaders before them.

———

A few in Canadian history do stand out in this way, namely as leaders who inspired great loyalty, support, affection, and respect.

When Sir John A. Macdonald died at the end of his remarkable career, the most eloquent and acute analysis of his gift for leadership was given by his political opponent, Wilfrid Laurier. In a speech that it is difficult to imagine a leader giving about an opponent these days, Laurier summed up Macdonald's qualities this way:

> For the supreme art of governing men, Sir John Macdonald was gifted as few men in any land or in any age were gifted—gifted with the most high [sic] of all qualities, qualities which would have made him famous wherever exercised, and which would have shone all the more conspicuously the larger the theatre.
>
> The fact that he could congregate together elements the most heterogeneous and blend them into one compact party, and to the end of his life keep them steadily under his hand, is perhaps altogether unprecedented. The fact that during all those years he retained unimpaired not only the confidence, but the devotion—the ardent devotion and affection of his party, is evidence that, besides those higher qualities of statesmanship to which we were the daily witnesses, he was also endowed with those inner, subtle, undefinable graces of soul which win and keep the hearts of men. . . . Although my political views compel me to say that, in my judgment, his actions were not always the best that could have been taken in the interest of Canada, although my conscience compels me to say that of late he has imputed to his opponents motives which I must say in my heart he has misconceived, yet I am only too glad here to sink these differences, and to remember only the

great services he has performed for our country—to re-member that his actions always displayed great originality of views, unbounded fertility of resources, a high level of intellectual conception, and, above all, a far-reaching vision beyond the event of the day, and still higher, permeating the whole, a broad patriotism—a devotion to Canada's welfare, Canada's advancement, and Canada's glory.

As Laurier pointed out, Macdonald loved power and loved being prime minister. But in order to achieve success, he had to go beyond himself to unite a fractious party and a fractured country, and he had to do it at all times with what has rightly been called "the inner graces of the soul." Today's Canada is a country similarly lacking in unity and purpose. Where, then, is the grace and intelligence shown by past leaders rising to such challenges? Why are we not holding our leaders more accountable and demanding that they replace character assassination with such respectful debate?

Closer to home and our own time, Pierre Trudeau captured Canadians' imaginations in a way that has much resonance to this day. As a young man in the '60s, I was inspired by his vision of a Canada with a Charter of Rights and a constitution we could call our own. Watching Trudeau in the House of Commons, it was hard not to be impressed with his engagement in debate, his full acceptance that the House was the sparring ground where he had to win the day. He could be charming when he wanted to be, but he did not always want to be. My sense from my opposition seat was that coming into politics in midlife, he remained a bit aloof from some of the exercise of the "inner graces" that Laurier described.

Macdonald, Laurier, and Mackenzie King were all lifers, starting in politics at an early age and sticking with political life right to the end of the road. It is a path much less followed today. Pierre Trudeau was a teacher, writer, and political activist, but he did not become a parliamentarian until his mid-forties. His rise to the top was dramatic; he became leader of the Liberal Party and prime minister just a few years after joining Lester B. Pearson's cabinet. Mr. Pearson himself was a career diplomat who was appointed to the cabinet as foreign minister before winning his Northern Ontario seat in a by-election. He was not an eloquent speaker or a visionary, but his skill as a leader was in getting things done. His time in office between 1963 and 1968 was probably the most productive five years in Canadian government history outside wartime—and he did it all with a minority government. His opponents mocked him as a bumbler, but his political skills allowed him to accomplish much without insisting on personal credit for his achievements.

Macdonald, Laurier, and Mackenzie King were all lifers, starting in politics at an early age and sticking with political life right to the end of the road. It is a path much less followed today.

Pierre Trudeau's leadership was of a different quality. Ironically, had he decided to retire after losing the May 1979 election to Joe Clark, historians would have a much different view of his talents and achievements than we do today. Such is the effect that fortune and timing can have on a leader's legacy. It was Trudeau's re-election in

1980 and his iron determination to proceed with the patriation of the Constitution with an entrenched Charter of Rights and Freedoms that continue to capture the imagination and support of Canadians. Like Churchill in 1940, Mr. Trudeau was the right man for the right issue.

Pierre Trudeau, Frank Scott, and Bora Laskin were friends in the 1950s and '60s, all three law professors and advocates of the need for a bill of rights and for Canada to have its own constitution. All took a dim view of how poorly civil rights were protected in Canadian law at the time and of the consequences of allowing the Constitution to remain a British Act of Parliament. They took an even dimmer view of how the British law lords had interpreted the Canadian Constitution and to what extent the powers of the federal government had been eroded by what they all saw as a perverse reading of the Canadian experience. In one of his poems, Frank Scott accused the Privy Council of "worshipping at the altar of divided jurisdiction."

Patriation of the Constitution happened after an exhaustive national discussion, and it was not an exercise in partisanship or of one person working in isolation. The same goes for the Charter. The origins of the desire to "bring the Constitution home" go back decades. The quest for a better protection for individual and group rights can be traced to all three major parties of the day—the NDP, the Progressive Conservatives, and the Liberals. John Diefenbaker, Ellen Fairclough, Gordon Fairweather, Tommy Douglas, David Lewis, and Ed Broadbent were just as much authors of the Charter as Pierre Trudeau and his lieutenant at the time, Jean Chrétien.

Still, given the messy implementation of the patriation plan, there can be no doubt that were it not for Pierre Trudeau, it would never have happened. But the image of Mr. Trudeau as unbending in all circumstances is not accurate. It is often forgotten that he had to make two major compromises in order to get constitutional reform done. The first was to accept important changes to the wording of the Charter, in particular as would recognize the need for stronger guarantees for equality rights, and to agree to the section 35 wording that upheld existing Aboriginal and treaty rights. In both cases, the changes have had a powerful impact on the interpretation of the Constitution by Canadian courts. Trudeau did not embrace these changes with enthusiasm but recognized them as the price of political success. He would not have won the support he needed from the New Democratic Party without them.

The second compromise revolved around Trudeau's acceptance of a notwithstanding clause that would allow Parliament and provincial legislatures to overrule a court decision. The Supreme Court's majority decision to draw a distinction between what was "the law" and what was "constitutional convention" forced Mr. Trudeau back to the negotiating table with the premiers. Both Premier Bill Davis of Ontario and Ed Broadbent, to my knowledge, argued strongly that a greater effort to find a consensus had to be made. When Pierre Trudeau was told that accepting the notwithstanding clause was the price for the support of those premiers who were still resisting patriation, he initially said, "No deal." But he could not afford to lose the support of Ontario, New Brunswick, or the federal NDP. In a clear indication of his efficacy as a leader, Trudeau compromised to broaden support for the package.

Without Pierre Trudeau's leadership, none of this would have been possible. He had a vision of what he wanted to have happen, but he operated in the political realities of the moment, aware of what he had to do to make it happen. If he had ignored the entreaties to stay on as leader of the Liberal Party in 1979, neither patriation nor the Charter of Rights would have even been on the agenda. And once they were, if Trudeau had refused to bend in his negotiations with the premiers, the enactment of both would never have come about. There can be no doubt that Trudeau's leadership—more specifically, his ability to be firm in his intentions but to compromise when necessary to ensure his vision became reality—altered the country profoundly.

———

Nostalgic reflection on the Constitution belies the truth that the process of patriation was a protracted, difficult affair. The behind-the-scenes work accomplished by Trudeau, the premiers, and the body of lieutenants and aides continued after Trudeau's government ended, and it was taken up again in earnest by Brian Mulroney.

Mulroney presented himself to the country as a better successor to Pierre Trudeau than John Turner. Campaigning with Bill Davis through the Ontario heartland, Mulroney let everyone know that social programs were safe and that the enlightened capacity for reform and change of the Big Blue Machine would soon be in place in Ottawa.

The campaign was not flawless. Dalton Camp's famous comment that Mulroney might be able to give up booze and cigarettes but couldn't shake hyperbole spoke to a Mulroney trait that would contribute mightily to the steady erosion of his public support—what seemed at first to be part of the blarney charm eventually gnawed away at his credibility. But that was only a cloud on the horizon in 1984. Mulroney's mandate in that year was a tribute to his skill at presenting himself as a moderate of the centre. In one of his earliest decisions, Mulroney, with one eye on history and another firmly on Quebec, made it clear that he was foursquare for bilingualism. He was not going to allow the Liberals to outflank him.

The negotiations in 1987 with the premiers on constitutional change also spoke to his strengths as a mediator. Mulroney's interpersonal skills were exceptional. He worked carefully with the freshly reminted Bourassa government to encourage Quebec to come forward with a limited number of constitutional changes. The premiers, meeting in Edmonton, agreed to a "Quebec Round" that would focus on these proposals and nothing else.

What followed was a triumph of Mulroney's negotiating skills—the deal would not likely have been done without him—and a failure of ratification. This failure was not due to a lack of leadership, but rather to factors outside of Mulroney's control. The lengthy process in Manitoba reflected the second thoughts of the Pawley government and its social democratic base. The elections of Frank McKenna in New Brunswick and Clyde Wells in Newfoundland were even more problematic.

It was the controversy over this Meech Lake Accord in 1987 that led to the unravelling of the coalition Mulroney had crafted. While he won a second mandate over the free trade issue, Mulroney's second term saw a collapse in his support as dramatic as John Diefenbaker's twenty-five years before, with Preston Manning stealing the populist underpinning right from under Mulroney's western support. Lucien Bouchard, who the prime minister had wooed and nurtured to join him in Ottawa, repaid the kindness by putting a large shiv between the prime minister's shoulder blades in 1990, an act of betrayal from which Mulroney never really recovered.

What this lead-up and fallout shows is that, sometimes, the issues with leadership have nothing to do with the leader themselves. Though an individual may have all of the strengths necessary to take on a task, the truth is that any leader can only control her own actions and not the reactions of others, let alone the host of external factors in which she must operate. Vision is important, but it cannot survive if it ignores or distorts reality.

———

There have been few entrances onto the political scene more dramatic than that of President Barack Obama. A community worker and law professor, the son of a black Kenyan father and a white American mother, Obama's rise to the presidency was truly meteoric. He served less than one full term in the U.S. Senate before taking on the anointed candidate of the Democratic Party establishment, Hillary Rodham Clinton.

To say he raised expectations with his eloquence would be an understatement. Few presidents have moved so many with their words. Yet the speeches of his 2008 campaign were matched by two other key things—the simplicity of his message ("Yes we can!") and the unprecedented use of technology and the enthusiasm of political volunteers in identifying and mobilizing supporters.

Obama's eloquence, and all the magic of the rallies that grew and grew in size, were enhanced by an organization whose toughness and focus led to the remarkable victory in the primaries, then in the general election against John McCain in 2008, and again in 2012 against Mitt Romney.

President Obama then suffered an ignominious defeat in the midterm elections of 2014, losing control of the Senate and even more seats in the House. Yet even that defeat was not the final word. His approval ratings sank to the low 40s, and he was asked by a great many Democrats to just stay away as they struggled to hold on to their seats in the House and the Senate. Not long after, a feistier Obama took executive action on immigration, communicating with more candour and directness, clearly feeling freer to speak his mind.

Obama's newfound frankness should not be surprising, given that his vision for his country—initially so welcome—is still being tested. He won the Democratic nomination in good part because he captured the fatigue of his party, and ultimately his country, with the wars in Iraq and Afghanistan. He speaks proudly of having brought troops home. But when faced with a dramatically deteriorating situation in the Middle East and elsewhere, he has been forced to re-engage militarily, albeit without troops on the ground, and has made unparalleled use of drones and targeted killings from the air to, in his words, "degrade and eventually defeat" a terrorist enemy.

In many ways, Obama is faced, as was Roosevelt, with attempting to lead a country that is caught between wanting the simplicity of peace and yet facing the complexity of conflict. Public opinion wants a quick defeat of the forces of terror, and yet most seasoned experts and analysts tell us that the conflict will be protracted and difficult. Similarly, on Iran, Republicans can rant about the framework for a nuclear deal, but they know full well the appetite in the electorate for military action against Iran is not there.

In these circumstances, there is always the temptation to tell the public what it wants to hear. This is a guarantee of current popularity at the risk of long-term ignominy. To pledge, for example, that there will not be a need for ground troops, or to set timetables for withdrawal that are more related to domestic politics than to military strategy, is unwise. The key test of policy is effectiveness within a moral compass and the rule of law. It is wrong to pretend that we can be more precise than that.

> *The key test of policy is effectiveness within a moral compass and the rule of law.*

The American economy is improving and growing; both unemployment and the deficit are coming down. No Republican leader has emerged with a galvanizing capacity to shape an alternative vision to that of the president. So how do we explain the trajectory of Comet Obama? The answer would appear to be that his greatest strength is also his weakness. The president has the power of words and an organizational ability that brought him twice to the presidency. But for leadership to be effective, the ability to describe the world has to be matched by the capacity to change it. The skill set that took him to the presidency has not always made him an effective president.

———

When Richard Nixon left office he quoted these words of Theodore Roosevelt: "It is not the critic who counts; not the man who points out how the strong man stumbles. . . . The credit belongs to the man who is actually in the arena, whose face is marred by dust and sweat and blood; who strives valiantly . . . who at the best knows in the end the triumph of high achievement, and who, at the worst, if he fails, at least fails while daring greatly."

At the unveiling of his official portrait in the House of Commons, Jean Chrétien made a similar point in defending the art of politics, saying, "This is a tough life, but it is a very noble life." Chrétien was proud of his long career as a member of Parliament and cabinet minister. He liked his fellow members of Parliament, and they liked him. He counted among his many friends members of the opposition, and he knew how to read the mood of a room and of the House. He also prided himself on knowing the character and ambitions of the people around him; he was under no illusions that politics is about anything but power, about winning it and keeping it.

He was, and is to this day, underestimated by both his rivals and his opponents. He cultivated the personality of being "le p'tit gars," the little guy, who grew up in a paper town called Shawinigan and who had no pretences. It was a persona and, while accurate as to his roots, it did not describe either his abilities or the extent of his ambition. He accomplished much by stealth and by the steady, systematic cultivation of support within his party. Losing the Liberal leadership to John Turner in 1984, he left politics for a few years to build a stronger financial base for himself and his family, but his love of the political game never left him, nor did his understanding of the need for organization and discipline to achieve what he wanted.

Timing is not everything, but it sure helps. Mr. Chrétien took office in 1993, just as the economy was starting to recover and slowly beginning to generate the jobs and revenue that allowed his government to reduce the deficit in dramatic fashion by the turn of the century. Led by the efforts of Chrétien and his rival Paul Martin, the minister of finance, the Liberals reduced transfers to the provinces and social programs, and then taxes, attempting to do so in a way that avoided the ideological enthusiasm of their opponents in the Reform Party.

Successful transitions of leadership are vital to the lasting success of any institution. Politics is about the accumulation and preservation of power, and one of the most difficult things for any leader to do is to recognize when it is time to develop a plan for succession.

The rivalry between John Turner and Jean Chrétien was well known, as was the later chafing between Chrétien and his eventual successor, Paul Martin. The process of transition in the Liberal leadership between 2001 and 2004 was messy, and as a newly minted member of the Liberal Party in 2006, my ears were filled with stories of perfidy and betrayal on all sides. A house divided cannot stand, and the country was sufficiently unimpressed with the bickering to give Stephen Harper a minority mandate in 2006 and to let the Liberal Party sort itself out in a series of leadership changes that happened four times between 2006 and 2013. The shift from Liberal to Conservative, and Mr Harper's methodical and unrelenting implementation of his agenda, have gradually but unmistakably brought about a very different Canada.

Leadership is never easy, but it is always necessary. Personality and policy, individual ambition and party strength, imagination and pragmatism—there are a host of considerations that must be balanced to make necessary changes possible. This high-wire exercise in control, patience, and planning can be made or unmade at any moment. My favourite comment on the challenges this poses to those brave enough to take on the mantle of leadership comes from Phil Givens, onetime mayor of Toronto. "Bobby baby, in this business you don't get what you deserve. You get what's coming to ya."

As events unfold, it will be fascinating to see what the political leaders of our own time have coming to them. As the air I breathe becomes less partisan, it is still possible to discern strengths and vulnerabilities on all sides. Stephen Harper was badly underestimated by his opponents and dismissed as being too stiff and too dogmatic. What this criticism missed, and still misses, is that he is determined, disciplined, and even pragmatic as he steers the country to where he thinks it should be. During the minority Parliaments after 2006, his government quickly spent the surpluses built up by the Liberals, cutting taxes at the same time. In cutting the Goods and Services Tax, Mr. Harper offended every economist in the country, but he was more interested in how ordinary Canadians reacted to what was, after all, an unpopular tax.

Mr. Harper has not inspired deep affection like a Ronald Reagan, but there is a respect from enough of the electorate to make it possible, though certainly not inevitable, for him to win another mandate. To the conservative agenda, one has to add the toughness of his party's attacks on his opponents. Both Stéphane Dion and Michael Ignatieff were the objects of ruthless, but it must be said effective, attacks, to which the Liberal Party was not able to respond. None of it was pretty, but fear can be as important a motivator in politics as it is in the rest of our lives. As the issue of security becomes more important in people's minds, the party and leader that offer the deepest sense of understanding and competence will win support. At the same time there is always the risk that negativity, fear, and nastiness may become issues in their own right. People may tire of it, wanting more optimism and more hope.

In many ways, Justin Trudeau is the polar opposite of Stephen Harper. He is charming, entering a room with enthusiasm and warmth, joking with the crowd. He has charisma. He likes people, and people like him. He is resilient. When he challenged Patrick Brazeau to a boxing match, many people (myself included) thought he had made a great mistake, risking his reputation for no good reason. We were wrong. The public identified with his bravado, and he showed a discipline and determination that had been underestimated.

The Conservative assault on Mr. Trudeau has just begun, with the belief that what worked on Stéphane Dion and Michael Ignatieff will work one more time. The Liberals tried shrugging it off before, but they will need a more effective response this time. Can Justin Trudeau describe a vision with enough details and practical elements to have broad public appeal? Will people tire of the negativity of his opponents, or will the attack ads have enough effect to discourage potential voters? With only two years of leadership under his belt, Justin Trudeau has done a commendable job of completing the rebuild of the Liberal Party and building a base of support. Even so, it will take an extraordinary campaign to put the Liberals in majority territory.

Canada hasn't had a two-party system since the end of the First World War, and the New Democratic Party no doubt feels that its breakthrough in the last election should leave them as real contenders in the next contest. But life isn't fair. Jack Layton's tragic death soon after the most successful federal election result for the NDP in history deprived the party of the man who was the catalyst for the breakthrough.

In the last three weeks of the 2011 campaign, voters in Quebec turned from the Bloc Québécois to the NDP without so much as a nod to the Liberals. This does not appear to have been a seismic shift to the left or right but rather a reaction to what was on offer at the time. As capable and effective a parliamentary performer as Tom Mulcair undoubtedly is, he is thus far having difficulty generating the warmth and affection that Jack Layton did and that Tommy Douglas and Ed Broadbent did before him. The NDP's success will depend on the election itself giving the party a chance to show that the substance of their platform and the competence of their leader can win increased support.

So a campaign will see Tom Mulcair, a man with no shortage of policy, trying to show a more human side and trying to prove that 2011 was no fluke. It will feature Justin Trudeau, a gifted persuader, working hard to show that his charm is a prologue to real leadership. And it will have Stephen Harper, a leader who can get things done, but causing deep division along the way, seeking a better connection with the electorate. But each leader's one strength will not be enough. Vision, persuasion, and implementation will all need to feature. The result may not be decisive, and a majority may prove elusive. But that could prove more of an opportunity to Canadians than they might think. If an election means that our leaders have to compromise, engage with one another as respected colleagues and opponents—rather than as caricatures to be derided and ignored—and work within the realities of the present day, it means they have to listen to the issues that Canadians bring forward. If not, and any one person is left to shape the country according to his or her own vision, then Canadians will have to ask: What will that vision entail?

CHAPTER THREE

WHAT'S HAPPENED TO POLICY?

At the outset of the federal election in 1993, Prime Minister Kim Campbell made a comment at once disarming in its honesty and depressing in its implications: "An election is a very bad time to be discussing serious issues of public policy." No doubt she was expressing thoughts that would have been drummed into her by every strategic advisor—after all, they would have told her, an election is about feelings, emotions, positioning, branding, targeting, polling, and repositioning, rebranding, and retargeting one more time. In that one brief sentence, Kim Campbell was not expressing contempt or disdain for the electorate but rather was saying what most people in the political business really think. She spilled the beans.

Twenty years later, the discussion of public policy both in and out of Parliament is more polarized and dysfunctional than ever. The decline of deference, the rise of celebrity (and the fall of these same celebrities as well), the shift to infotainment, the explosion in the frequency and range of media coverage—these all contribute to the perception of politics as a circus and distract from the truly important matters, namely the specific legislation our government is enacting and how it goes about doing so.

It has been said that good public policy is what happens when all the alternatives have been exhausted. But what happens if Canadians' patience wears out waiting for that to happen?

Demographers tell us that population is everything. They're not far wrong, at least when it comes to policy creation. Take the example of the baby boomers, whose lives have determined the policy focus of governments for the past seven decades. In the early 1950s, the largest item in Ontario's budget was transportation—think of the Toronto subway, the construction of Highway 400 to Barrie, the Don Valley Parkway, or the last link of the Trans-Canada Highway being laid in northern Ontario in 1960. It was the birth of suburbia, and as the baby boomer contingent grew older, the money followed, with the spending on education quickly outgrowing that on transportation as the baby boomers entered the school system. With the national decision to embrace Medicare in the 1970s, health spending by governments grew accordingly.

We are now at the point when the baby boom generation is confronting its golden years. When Otto von Bismarck, then the chancellor of Germany, set the age of retirement at sixty-five in 1889, life expectancy was well below that. Not anymore. People are working later into life as they consume pensions and health care. There are several growing cohorts among the baby boomers—young old, middle-aged old, and the frail elderly. Each has differing needs, demands, and perspectives, many of which are dictating the particular policy being created. The danger with this is that it neglects the younger populations who will have to bear the future costs and weight of the decisions being made in the present.

This is not so much about bigger or smaller government as it is about the capacity of all governments to be able to adjust current entitlement financing to allow for more spending on the future, on infrastructure, on child care and family support, and on education. It requires an honest recognition of the obligations each generation owes to the others, and to those whose time will come. It is about encouraging a real discussion on the possibility of Canada (as it did in the 1850s, the early 1900s, and in the postwar years) setting out to allow its population to grow at an even faster rate with higher rates of immigration and, at the same time, to shift our economic and energy growth to a genuinely sustainable path.

We are all facing a retirement crunch, a pension crunch, and a health care crunch. More broadly, Canadians, especially the younger population, have to confront the fact that governments (and individuals) have indulged current spending at the expense of long-term investment. And so we are met with some basic questions of intergenerational equity. What is the best approach to righting Canada's economy and positioning it for long-term success in a global context? How can we ensure that Canada improves its environmental sustainability, preserving our land and its riches for generations to come? And how can we keep our population healthy as our Medicare system faces an increasingly heavy burden?

When it comes to what effect governmental policy will have on them, many Canadians understandably look first to the economy. Canadians of every type have financial concerns that need to be addressed through substantial, deep-rooted change. Taking stock of how we've reached our current state sheds some light on what is needed to bring us back to where we need to be.

In the late fall of 2008, Jim Flaherty, whose death came far too soon, brought forward an economic statement that should have led to the downfall of the Harper government—he drastically underestimated both the depth of the economic crisis taking place around him and the risks of being in a minority government. The forecasts in that document never happened, and a balanced budget became a $55 billion deficit in the blink of an eye. He kept his job and lived to see a surplus on the horizon, but again, this was for reasons that lay beyond the power of prediction.

The "oil experts" and "the consensus of bank economists" have been assuring policymakers for the last several years that oil prices would stay high for the present and the future, because demand would stay strong with Asian economies booming. Changes on the supply side, as well as a game of chicken between Middle Eastern and North American producers, have lowered prices by 50 percent. It's possible that when this game of who blinks first is over, or some other political crisis unfolds, prices will go back up, but who knows when or by how much?

Canadians are fixated on who the winners and losers of this game will be in Canada, but we need to lift our heads a bit and take stock of where we stand in the bigger picture. Russia's falling ruble and the debt crisis of its elites and their companies have rightly grabbed headlines. But a couple of countries, notably Nigeria and Venezuela, are now in political crisis, and their very stability is at risk in the days ahead.

A healthy dose of reality and scepticism is always a good idea.

One of the implications of the 2008–09 world economic crisis is that regional and world institutions have much less room to manoeuvre and help sort things out. When a Greek election produces another mess for the European Union and the International Monetary Fund, and oil dependent economies face collapse with major political consequences, it will be harder for those agencies to do as much as is required. Stability doesn't come cheap.

I am far from being a doom and gloom prognosticator. But a healthy dose of reality and scepticism is always a good idea. In a useful piece of advice, Rudyard Kipling reminded us that triumph and disaster are both impostors. People draw too many conclusions from current trends. They fail to understand that trends can change and that, above all, events can get in the way.

All of this speaks to the need for some humility, particularly in the ranks of the pundits. But this is also a time for courage, because politics needs to stretch the art of the possible. Telling majorities what they want to hear will get us nowhere.

By 2008, the enthusiasm for deregulation and an explosion

of greed led to a banking crisis, which in turn led to a fiscal crisis, which in turn meant an even deeper banking crisis, followed by a jobs crisis. Canada was not immune from the massive downturn that hit the United States and Europe. A Conservative government that preached nothing but restraint and austerity found itself spending tens of billions of borrowed money to offset the unemployment and unused capacity that had infected the national economy.

The recent financial crisis in the United States and Europe brings all these experiences to bear. Some are arguing that austerity and restraint are the panacea for the world economy. But this in fact ignores the lessons from the '90s—that righting of the ship depends on growth and strong revenues, as well as the political will to make change happen. A continued forced march to austerity when there is no growth can make matters worse, not better.

No serious person would argue that deficits and debts are anything but a challenge and a problem. Indeed, looking at the European situation, it would appear that even deeper restructurings will be needed to restore confidence and get things back on track. But heroic targets have to be matched by a sense of both political and economic realism. Growth and jobs are what give people hope, optimism, and a greater willingness to make difficult decisions.

Growth and jobs are what give people hope, optimism, and a greater willingness to make difficult decisions.

Investing in infrastructure, education, and innovation makes good sense. While no country can successfully stimulate on its own (another lesson from the '90s), all governments have to be prepared to look at both the spending side and the revenue side to deal effectively with their problems. And no one can ignore that cuts made without matching growth, or cuts that fall unfairly on lower income groups alone, can have disastrous social and political consequences.

Tea Party economics is based on a simplistic theory that taxes are evil and that to reduce public spending is, at all times and in all places, a universal good. Some are so mesmerized by these theories that they see no choice but to succumb to "Teapartynomics," quibbling only about the degree of slashing required. We should find the political will and voice to remind ourselves that sustainable growth and well-paying jobs, the creation of wealth, and the sharing of opportunity for the present and the future are the real objectives, and that policies on taxing and spending have to answer the simple question: Will this decision help make us richer, help share opportunity, and protect future generations? There is a progressive answer to this question, and it's important to get it right.

Oliver Wendell Holmes once rightly said that "taxes are the price we pay for civilization," but that sentiment is rarely expressed much these days. Parties of the left are prepared to repeat the mantra "tax the rich," but the evidence is overwhelming that the revenues produced by these measures would be paltry compared to what it will, in fact, take to ensure a broader sharing of the prosperity that the world economy is generating for a powerful minority of people.

The evidence that the bonds of solidarity and shared experience—which should be the hallmark of economic and social democracies—have unravelled is overwhelming. The extent of the inequality is powerful and of much greater significance than it has been at any time since the 1930s. While inequalities of some kind are inevitable, their extent and persistence are a matter of choice. At critical points in economic history, policies have shifted to address the worst inequities. The rise of unionism and social policies like workers' compensation, unemployment insurance, progressive taxation, and the regulatory state were all intended to inject a degree of democracy and human control over the excesses of their day. These forces, and the arguments for them, seem weaker today than at any point in the last hundred years. The growth of inequality threatens the fabric of Canadian society, and a sclerosis in social mobility threatens people's sense of fairness and opportunity. Describing the problem forces us to look harder at what can be done to address it.

Some clear directions need to be set out. The first is a willingness to address the gaps in affordable access to child care and early childhood education, housing, drugs and homecare, and post-secondary education. Sometimes these issues are conflated to mean universal, state-run provisions, but that is not always the best way to proceed. The point is to ensure access for everyone, to make sure no one is left out or falls behind, and to ensure that all providers are complying with standards that are fairly set and well monitored. The second is to recognize that innovation in the economy will increasingly be a key driver of growth. The third is

Evidence and measurement should be the guide of policy, not ideology or the self-interest of those who benefit from one way of doing things.

to use market tools, like pricing, to drive public policy more effectively.

Evidence and measurement should be the guide of policy, not ideology or the self-interest of those who benefit from one way of doing things. There must be a willingness to assess the outcomes of programs in order to allow change to happen. There is a complacency and sense that nothing much can be done because of the power of impersonal forces. This is the first thing to be overcome. The second is the notion that simply talking about the issue solves it. We need to be prepared to take steps, without throwing our understanding of the economy out the window. It's not an easy balance to strike, but we have no choice.

Growing up, many of us had a certain picture of Canada in our heads. A country of limitless resources, clean lakes, and vast forests, nature's bounty our inheritance as citizens of a land blessed with enormous wealth. It is a picture based in good part on reality. We can trace the history of our country through the search for resource wealth. The first peoples of Canada travelled with the resources and settled where they were most plentiful. Long before the permanent settlements in Nova Scotia and Quebec, European fishermen came to the Grand Banks for the greatest fishery they had ever seen. They were followed by those seeking fur and a passage to Asia, and on it went: lumber, gold, silver, and the twentieth-century search for uranium and oil.

There are some who see this resource wealth as a curse, even a disease. This is simplistic nonsense. It is an important part of who we are, a great advantage for Canada. But the extent of that advantage is up to each generation of Canadians. Like anything that is given to us, it can be exploited for short-term gain and then squandered. Some will try to get rich quick and be left with little in the bank at the end. "Rip it and ship it" is a recipe for disaster.

As a country our geographical size belies another reality—Canada is an international country whose economy is deeply dependent on trade. The money each of us has in his pocket, wherever we work, depends on what's happening in world markets. This is true for every country in the world today, but few more so than Canada. Economic policy must be drafted with this thought always in mind.

As a relatively small, trade-dependent economy, we need a rules-based, law-based trading system to keep the bigger players from throwing their weight around. This also means that, as a smaller economy, we have to be careful about how we negotiate bilateral deals. When we engage with China, Europe, and India, we need to understand the imbalance of power and how resistant large parts of these economies are to real competition. Whether it's the Europeans insisting on their patent rules applying to us or the Chinese wanting free access without granting us real reciprocity, we must not give away too much.

We have to go into all these discussions with our eyes wide open. Free trade is like a cold shower—everyone says how good it is for you but not everyone takes one. From agricultural subsidies to industrial incentives, we need to be aware that all our trading partners are good at lecturing us, but not so good at being pure themselves, and often for good, domestic reasons.

Development has to work for people as well as corporations. It needs to be on a human scale and a human pace, and it needs to respect the fact that much of the development of our energy and economic potential is taking place in parts of the country to which the Aboriginal peoples have an important claim.

The pace and extent of development has to respect something else as well, and that is the growing realization over the last fifty years that the air we breathe and the water we drink are, in fact, borrowed from our children. Polluting the environment creates deficits of unknown proportions for future generations. Canada has obligations—to itself, to the world, and to those who will follow us—to ensure that its development is sustainable.

If sustainable development is to be more than an empty phrase, several things must happen.

1. Subsidies on fossil fuels have to end, and more aggressive action has to be taken to reduce carbon emissions, not just in the oil sands, but everywhere. For starters, this means putting a price on carbon, as some provinces—Alberta, British Columbia, and Quebec—have clearly done. If governments were to price carbon and other forms of pollution properly, they would be less vulnerable to oil and other shocks. They would also be encouraging a shift to alternative ways of producing energy. It is telling that Premier Wynne's campaign team must have drawn the lesson from Stéphane Dion's defeat in 2008 that however meritorious

Subsidies on fossil fuels have to end.

the green shift really is, it is more something governments *do* rather than something political parties campaign *to do* during an election.

2. The federal government has to take the lead in consultations with all the Aboriginal communities who will be affected by energy development—from Muskrat Falls to the Yukon—and ensure that they have real participation in the development of these resource fields and in reaping its dividends. The provinces have to engage in this discussion of sharing resource revenues. Quebec showed the way in its James Bay Agreements and two subsequent accords, but other governments need to push for understandings that are based on partnership and not conquest.

3. The federal government needs to lead a discussion on the infrastructure—from power lines to pipelines—that will be needed to get sustainable energy to markets at home and abroad. The Harper government talks about staying away from making market decisions. If they would look at their own past, they would realize that Macdonald, Borden, Bennett, Diefenbaker, and Mulroney would never have fallen into such ideological rhetoric. Markets are institutions we must respect, but they should not become the object of religious veneration.

4. The federal government should be accelerating its investment in carbon reduction, capture, and storage, sending a clear signal on carbon pricing to the oil companies (as they themselves have requested) to unleash the necessary private investment in alternative energy.

5. Governments should maintain incentives for wind, solar, and geothermal investment by individuals and companies

and reinstate incentives to homeowners to encourage home energy efficiency.

In short, development without full participation in sustainable practices is simply no longer possible.

A sustainable national energy strategy can also be a source of well-paying jobs across the full breadth of the economy. From infrastructure and construction to advanced manufacturing, the job potential is huge. This is what makes pitting the old economy against the new economy, or resources against manufacturing so wrongheaded. But it will also take a real industrial strategy—with lower taxes on manufacturing and deeper incentives for research and innovation—as well as a coordinated skills strategy to ensure that we achieve the full advantage of our potential. There are still barriers to entry to skilled trades, bottlenecks between colleges and universities. We're too slow to get young people into apprenticeships and too slow to get them qualified. Apprentices are often the last hired and the first fired. The average age of an apprentice in Germany is seventeen; in Ontario it's twenty-seven. We can't let provincial jurisdiction stop real cooperation and mobility.

> *A sustainable national energy strategy can also be a source of well-paying jobs across the full breadth of the economy.*

Naomi Klein's recent much-heralded book, *This Changes Everything*, argues that the issue is "the environment versus capitalism" and uses climate change and pollution as yet another argument for, well, socialism.

The problem with this argument is that it confuses and conflates in the effort to persuade. Reducing waste, pollution, and carbon emissions are all good and necessary things. But they are not an argument against markets in and of themselves. They are an argument against markets that fail to price pollution (what the economists call an externality) properly.

The communist economies of the twentieth century were grossly polluting economies, embedded as they were in the culture of industrialism. The collapse of the Iron Curtain revealed rotting, corrupt structures where a small elite had great privileges, where control of the state benefitted a blessed few, and where industrial production was worshipped like never before. The Aral Sea in central Russia should become a poster child for environmental abuse and neglect, where uncontrolled industrial farming, use of pesticides, and systematic abuse of a freshwater inland sea has effectively destroyed it.

The conclusion is quite simple—uncontrolled growth and a failure to price the costs of this growth have been disastrous in capitalist countries just as surely as they have in communist countries.

The enemy is not capitalism. It is pollution. When societies fail to price the costs of growth properly, when they fail to regulate, fail to prosecute, and fail to innovate, when cronyism and favouritism become the rule rather than corrupt evils to be rooted out, problems are sure to follow.

The enemy is not capitalism. It is pollution.

Societies that value industrial development and the accumulation of wealth above all else are out of balance with nature. So, yes, global capitalism in its current state—with many governments too weak or corrupt to be able to regulate and protect the public interest—is a big problem. But since the middle of the nineteenth century, the argument that capitalism is so evil that only socialism will do as an antidote has led many countries to what must be described as a dead end, with only more pollution and chemical waste to show for it.

The key to finding better remedies is candour in admitting the difficulties. Enterprises that pollute—whether public or private—also create jobs and wealth. A remark that is attributed to Billie Holiday, among others, expresses a simple insight: "I've been rich and I've been poor and rich is better." The vast network of wealth production and distribution that we call an economy is not a simple thing, a switch to be turned on and off again at will. Nor are the choices to be made in regulating and guiding that economy—"steering rather than rowing"—always so simple.

When the United Nations issued the Brundtland Report more than twenty-five years ago in an effort to unite countries in the pursuit of sustainable development, one wag observed that in the phrase "sustainable development," environmentalists only got the adjective, not the noun. If the phrase had been "innovative sustainability," the perceived balance might have been different.

But if indeed the watchword is sustainability—to ensure that we produce wealth and run our societies in such a way that we don't take out more than we put back in—then that changes politics. Political leaders will have to be prepared to share a vision, and then a plan, and work in collaboration with others to make the plan happen. But this would mean making issues important before, during, and after an election.

If the political process, and the media fog that surrounds it, are not able to generate the decisions that are now needed more than ever, it will fall to an active citizenry, colleges and universities, nongovernmental organizations, and others to frame the debate and make change happen.

During one of my trips to Israel, I spent some time trying to understand how such a small country, facing so many different challenges, could become such a huge leader in innovation and the digital economy. The Start-Up Nation has something to teach the world, and Canada, in this department. What has taken place there needs to find more resonance here at home. The elements of success would seem to be these: The first is a commitment to education and the pursuit of knowledge from an early age. Early childhood education, literacy, and numeracy are a must. Unfortunately, present-day Canada is well behind the OECD averages in these departments. The second is a deep commitment to science education for both women and men, again starting at an early age and persisting through university and beyond. The third is public policies committed to embracing innovation, change, start-ups, and venture capital formation. Canada lags here as well, although there are some signs of successful clusters in centres across the country.

Those who say the answer lies in less government and lower taxes and then just stop there are actually wrong. The Israeli government invests directly in high tech without necessarily trying to pick winners and losers. It insists the private sector join it in taking risks. And it has a robust tax system.

Even more important is the nurturing of an entrepreneurial culture. One Israeli businessman said—in a phrase I found at once enlightening and comforting—"Failure is an event and not a person." The sense that things can happen, that the odds can be beaten, and that the job has to get done—these are all deeply ingrained in Israeli culture. Are they equally so in Canada?

———

What is true for innovative sustainability in making our economies work is also true for another touchstone of Canadian public policy: health care. A typical news story tells us of a man dying of a heart attack at his front door on a freezing night in Winnipeg. How could a bureaucracy be so thoughtless? A hospital spokesman dutifully announces that "policy will be changed" and that from now on the hospital and the taxi driver will make sure that after your discharge, you get through your front door before the taxi drives away. Problem solved? Hardly.

People (for the most part older people) are being pushed out of hospitals more quickly because there are no beds and no rooms for them. This is happening because too many patients are stuck in hospital beds when they should be receiving longer term care either at home or in a facility. Emergency room care and corridors chock full of people needing a real bed are not the exceptions in Canada today—they have become the rule.

It is generally conceded that hospitals do a reasonably good job of dealing with urgent, catastrophic problems. But waiting lists for longer term problems, like arthritic joint replacements or the time it takes to see a specialist, coupled with the lack of access to family practitioners in many parts of the country, speak to a broader problem. Frail, elderly people would prefer to stay at home, if at all possible. But the network of homecare is patchy and puts financial strains on them and their families.

Accessible care and necessary treatments on a timely basis as we get older are mainly private, not public, costs, as are the questions of where to live and how to get the appropriate level of attention. Drug care is not universal, and neither is dental care. Mental health costs are also largely borne by individuals and their families. The 1960s Medicare social contract, important as it is, is not just frayed at the edges—every year it covers less of the real cost to families.

After a flurry of concern about health care at the national level—the Liberal government's ten-year "fix it for a generation" plan in 2004 and Mr. Harper's "wait care guarantee" in 2006—the federal government has preferred to ignore completely issues surrounding the delivery of care. And so the burden of doing, or not doing, something falls on provinces, cities, private businesses, and above all, on families.

The great success of our system can be found in the millions of people who've been diagnosed and treated quickly and effectively without once being asked about their coverage or their income. Someone who is sick gets treatment, and serious illnesses get attention without people having to suffer anxiety about how they will pay.

But, increasingly, international comparisons are forcing us to admit that our system is far from perfect, that wait times for seeing a doctor or getting into treatment are simply not the best in the world, and that there are many costs of treatment that are not covered.

If the United States falters in its quest for a better system after the introduction of Obamacare, it will be their loss. It will also run counter to what a significant majority of Americans (like Canadians) really feel. Should anyone be denied health care because of her income, disability, or illness? No. Should patients be able to choose their doctors and advocate for speedy, effective treatment? Yes. Should insurers, taxpayers, and premium payers be worried about how to control costs as an ageing society combines with great technological advances to produce an expensive mix? Yes.

We should be proud of what we have, but we need to keep the focus on how to improve it; how to combine access, excellence, and innovation. We shouldn't treat health care as some kind of icon, a taboo subject too sacred to be discussed. We should keep what we have and make it better, as well as hope that our friends in the United States will find their own answers to the questions that lie at the heart of health care everywhere.

The deep partisanship that has marked the crisis in the U.S. Congress has some lessons for Canadians. Polarization should not be the new normal. It corrodes the body politic and takes us away from the fact that most people want a moderate, intelligent politics that's based on evidence, good values, and compromise.

Most Canadians do not actually want a viciously partisan left-right divide in this country.

The red-blue, right-left split in America makes bipartisanship almost impossible and has taken that country to an entirely avoidable brink. Most Canadians do not actually want a viciously partisan left-right divide in this country. The country has not suddenly turned hard right.

We need to remember that most goals in politics, as they are in hockey or soccer, are scored from the centre. That's where the action is, and that's where most Canadians are. This is not a dead centre but an action-filled, resilient, and lively place that is not afraid of ideas, debate, and looking at issues afresh.

So parties need to engage in a serious dialogue with Canadians about what a better health care system could look like and how it could be paid for. The moral commitment that is tied up with the decision to establish a national health care system in the 1970s, based on Saskatchewan's breakthrough a decade earlier, dealt with two major costs facing families: hospitalization and care from doctors.

Costs were to be shared fifty-fifty between the federal government and the provincial government. But as federal deficit spending grew in the 1970s, the Trudeau government insisted on limiting its financial exposure to growing costs. Through the Established Programs Financing Act (note that the bill was named before governments like Mike Harris's and Stephen Harper's started playing the Orwellian game of giving bills newspeak monikers like Ending House Arrest for Property and Other Serious Crimes by Serious and Violent Offenders Act), the government committed to a five-year funding cycle that would have to be renewed upon its expiry.

The provinces, in turn, attempted to limit their own costs by negotiating fees with medical associations while still allowing doctors to charge extra by using their own collective or individual fee schedules and having the patient bear the freight. This practice of extra billing became widespread and was eventually brought to an end by Monique Bégin's Canada

Health Act in 1984, when the federal government cut transfers to provinces that still allowed the practice. The Peterson Accord government followed suit after it came into office in 1985.

When Canadian federal and provincial governments decided that using the credit card to finance current spending was no longer tenable—with provincial governments leading the way in 1992, and Jean Chrétien's government following in the budget of 1994—health care budgets were naturally affected (although not as much as other parts of government spending, like housing, which was eventually smashed to smithereens).

In the early 2000s, two national studies—the Romanow Commission (also known as the Commission on the Future of Health Care in Canada) and the Kirby Report—focused attention once again on health care. Both called for a renewed role for the federal government. Romanow's suggestions focused on more federal cash coupled with more accountability for results and best practices. The cash part was relatively easy since those were boom times financially for both federal and provincial governments. The ten-year agreement signed by Paul Martin and the premiers in 2004 led to a steady increase in federal transfers to the provinces but less than spectacular results on structural change or dealing with the big gaps in funding for at-home care and drug costs.

The Kirby Report is rightly remembered for its focus on mental health, an area long ignored by all governments.

While visiting Kuujjuaq in the far north of Quebec a couple of years ago, my wife, Arlene, and I visited the local high school and saw a colourful mural on a wall dedicated to the memory of three students who had taken their own lives. On the wall in the gym we saw a huge declaration, "I Promise to Live," signed by their classmates. It was a stark reminder that suicide rates in Inuit communities are eleven times higher than in the general population.

Over a hundred years ago, the French sociologist Emile Durkheim wrote his groundbreaking book on suicide, reminding the world that while it is an act of individual despair, it has to be understood as a social phenomenon, with causes and consequences that go beyond the personal tragedy.

The suicide rate in Canada is higher today than in the 1950s. It is past time that we bring it out of the shadows. Let me suggest some critical elements of a national strategy.

We have to situate suicide in the broader context of mental health. The stigma associated with any illness of the mind is even greater for suicide. There are seventy people a week who take their own lives and hundreds more who try. The stigma of shame and isolation is still with us, as is the lie that these are issues of purely personal and private responsibility for which there is no real cure.

We have, in fact, made huge strides in treatment of mental health, but it remains a deep crisis for our society.

We have, in fact, made huge strides in treatment of mental health, but it remains a deep crisis for our society. One in five Canadians is directly affected. Tens of billions of dollars are lost to the economy. A patchwork quilt of volunteers and centres with inadequate resources and funding will not do.

This is another area where Canada is a laggard, not a leader.

We simply don't invest the resources in detection, in treatment, in jobs, in housing, in research, in breaking down the walls and barriers. Other countries do a better job, invest more, help more, cure more. We need to move from a culture of despair and neglect to one of hope. It takes more than words to do that; it takes a national strategy and, yes, it takes money.

The debates and discussions around this issue have changed substantially, and positively, since I entered public life over thirty-five years ago. But we still have a long way to go. While the stigma in public opinion has diminished, it has not disappeared. Treatments have improved dramatically, but individuals and families still face coping with the worlds of autism, depression, schizophrenia, and a wide range of other disorders without the deep assurance that in every instance we know what causes it and we know how to make it better. But more people are recovering, and better treatments are being found every day.

The debate in the House of Commons in 2012 on the need for a national suicide strategy was an eye-opening experience. Members came forward to share their own experiences; there was no name-calling, partisan chippiness, or the usual antics that go with a House debate. There was a sense that we are all in this together.

So that was progress. The next step is to match the words with even more deeds. There is a desperate shortage of help out there, and families with children all too often feel they are on their own. It will take a greater commitment of dollars and resources to make things happen, and that's harder to do in tough times. But it can and must be done.

Mental health is the weakest link in our health care system, but more important it is still the issue that hides away from conversation. There are still too few places outside a health care setting where the issue is addressed, as if mental health and addiction are still taboos not to be mentioned in polite company. Families wrestle with the need for privacy, but this can create a secret that needs to be hidden away, often with devastating consequences.

> *Mental health is the weakest link in our health care system, but more important it is still the issue that hides away from conversation.*

There are many places in our society that are suffering from the deep stress of abuse, violence, depression, and the torment of fear and loss. Not just people, but places. We put our soldiers in harm's way and then fail them when they respond like human beings to the full horror of war. We pass the wine and cheese while tut-tutting about poverty and dysfunction on First Nations reserves but have no strategy to deal with their awful consequences.

There are more voices speaking up than ever before, from the Mental Health Commission to Bell Canada to outspoken individuals across the spectrum of public life; we are further ahead today than twenty years ago. But we have miles to go before we sleep. The more taboos we can break the better off we are.

———

In the parliamentary debates of the future, is it possible to imagine that basic issues about our economy, our environment, and our social programs will be addressed at all? It should be, but it will only happen if voters, the press, the academic commentators, and responsible media refuse to accept pop as a permanent diet. Canada is less innovative than it needs to be, less green, less equal, and shows fewer sightings of public imagination and solidarity than would be healthy for all of us. We are not alone in this, but the fact that the weakness of our democratic pulse is shared by other countries should hardly be a source of consolation, let alone pride.

It will increasingly be left to a serious dialogue between and among Canadians young and old, well off and insecure, to wrestle with these questions we confront as a country. While the three ps of parliamentary politics—pandering, personal attack, and partisanship—dominate Question Period, we shall have to find a way to make sure the conversation happens and the right decisions are made.

It will increasingly be left to a serious dialogue between and among Canadians young and old, well off and insecure, to wrestle with these questions we confront as a country. While the three *p*s of parliamentary politics—pandering, personal attack, and partisanship—dominate Question Period, we shall have to find a way to make sure the conversation happens and the right decisions are made. No longer can we leave these decisions in the hands of Parliament. The tendency of politicians to deflect important policy considerations to a later date has become an epidemic. Regardless of their political affiliation, all Canadians—especially young ones—should be asking themselves, if policies are being drafted without their input and without their needs in mind, what burden will they be left to carry when the policymakers are gone?

CHAPTER FOUR

WHAT'S HAPPENED TO ABORIGINAL PEOPLES IN CANADA?

The fastest growing population in Canada is indigenous people. Their birth rate on reserves and in cities is high, and as children finish primary school, the exodus to urban centres picks up. In my work as an advocate for the First Nations in Ontario, I have seen that the federal government is not worried about that fact, because they interpret the constitutional responsibility for "Indians and lands reserved for Indians" in s.91 of the Constitution in the narrowest way and so pay scant attention, outside the blunt instrument of the criminal law, to what is happening in the major growth centres.

There was a time, not so long ago, when it was thought that Aboriginal people would disappear completely. The

1923 Williams Treaties in Ontario between the Crown and the Mississauga and Chippewa literally contained an "extinction clause." This dictated that whatever land and money was awarded to these Aboriginal people under the treaty had to be returned to the province of Ontario once the Aboriginal people disappeared.

Back at first contact in the sixteenth century, there were as many as 2 million people living in what is now Canada. European diseases decimated the population through one plague after the next. Add the violence that accompanied the new colonialism, and by 1871 the census only reported 100,000 Aboriginal people in Canada.

The government's plan was to bring that number to zero by assimilation. For a long time, the Indian Act dictated that any recognized Indian would lose status by voting, receiving a university degree, serving in the military, becoming a clergyman or lawyer, or marrying a non-native or non-status person. Death by a thousand clauses, or so the plan went.

It failed, not least because of the tremendous resilience of Aboriginal communities. In 2014, there were about 1.4 million Aboriginal Canadians, and given that population's consistently high birth rate, that number is swelling rapidly.

This trend will only grow, and the education, social service, and health care costs are, again, taken up by someone else further down the line.

The implications of this population boom were widely discussed by the Royal Commission on Aboriginal Peoples in the 1990s and then promptly ignored. The one emphatic response of the last decade—Paul Martin's Kelowna Accord, negotiated for over a year between Aboriginal leaders, the federal cabinet, and the provinces—was scrapped days after Mr. Harper took office. Its replacement has dramatically increased the incarceration rate among Aboriginal people and made an attempt to deal with the education agenda, and scant else. Mr. Harper gave an eloquent apology for the truly disastrous and racist policy of forcing First Nations children into residential schools, but the government never followed those words with the actions that would show any seriousness of purpose.

For all the rhetoric about nation building, the unresolved relationship between indigenous people and other Canadians and their governments stands out emphatically as nothing less than our national shame.

———

Attawapiskat is an impoverished, remote community on James Bay where most of the community is unemployed and most of the budget comes in the form of handouts from Ottawa. The amount of the money granted to the community is controlled by bureaucrats and politicians in Ottawa, who can change or stop it at any time. It is a classic colonial arrangement.

Attawapiskat is not the only community with such an arrangement—there are over six hundred bands across Canada that are covered by the Indian Act. For most of them, housing is a major concern, and with money in short supply, they are little prepared to deal with the problems they face.

But there is a third, underlying crisis beyond poverty and beyond housing—a crisis of governance. Municipal and Aboriginal governments share the problem that they have neither the means nor the powers to address the challenges that their citizens face, with the result that they are in a state of dependency on the federal government, with all the resentment and dysfunction that brings.

The solution rests in a new fiscal arrangement that ensures the right revenue streams go to the right levels of government, complete with all the transparency, responsibility, and accountability citizens want and need. Where there is corruption and waste, we must root it out, but colonialism is no way to govern.

Canada is an Aboriginal country as well as a settler country. We rarely see ourselves this way, but it is past time that we started doing so. The fact that settlers are in a significant majority does not take away from the simple fact that when Europeans made first contact with the northern half of North America, there were millions of people already here.

From the Beothuk in Newfoundland—a population completely wiped out by disease and violence—across every corner of Canada to the far west and north, Canada's first people had built a civilization, a way of life thousands of years old and rich in diversity. They were not "savages" (as they were called, in French and English), nor were they "ignorant wretches," nor were they less than people. They had developed complex societies with distinct languages, systems of governance; they were real people with a real way of life.

The first centuries after initial contact were marked by apocalyptic disease, racism, and colonial duplicity that promised peace and security and delivered neither.

The premise of colonial settlement was that the lands of the Americas were there to be conquered and populated as a matter of right. From a legal standpoint, the lands were described as *terra nullius*—"no-man's-land"—and therefore belonging to whichever empire could enforce its control through superior force of arms. From the earliest days, the accounts of the time tell us of the discrepancy between the worldview of the indigenous people and that of the Europeans. Land could not be given away or surrendered because it was not the indigenous people's to give—a gift of the creator could be shared, but it could not be sold. To the settlers, these ideas were incomprehensible. Land needed to be divided, worked, and controlled. It had to belong to someone.

When the British Empire took control of the French Empire's North American territories in 1763, the Treaty of Paris was quickly followed by the Royal Proclamation of 1763. It was a true expression of British "statecraft." Just as the Quebec Act eleven years later was about securing the loyalty of French Canadians in the face of trouble in the thirteen colonies, the British knew that they had to recognize the integrity of indigenous societies in order to deal with the appetite for settlement and expansion that was such a powerful feature of North American society.

As settlers in both British North America and the United States were granted more autonomy, the rights of the First Nations were increasingly dismissed. Gone were the noble ideas of peoples who, in the language of the Royal Proclamation, had a right "not to be molested or disturbed." Lands were given and then taken away; promises were made and then broken; people were moved at will. In the words of the 1763 Royal Proclamation, "Great frauds and abuses were committed."

But the frauds and abuses did not stop when King George III ordered them to end. In Canada, as in the rest of the Americas, the colonial process of settlement had the effect of dispossessing Aboriginal people, of moving them, of even killing them.

It is hard for us, today, to absorb the extent to which institutionalized racism was at the heart of public policy for so long in our own country, but it is something that we must acknowledge and remedy.

By the middle of the nineteenth century, it was a misguided conceit of public opinion that the "inferiority" of the indigenous people would lead to their disappearance. The Papal bulls of the sixteenth century that sanctified the invasion of the Americas had their Protestant equivalent, and the revival of the evangelical movement led to renewed efforts to convert the Aboriginal people and to subvert native customs and languages. The sheer number of settlers, their hunger for land, timber, and mineral wealth, led to a demand that reserve lands be broken up as much as possible and that the "illiterate and savage" population be kept apart.

As if this racism needed further support, social Darwinism was added to the mix. A new social science was emerging in Europe and the United States in which the idea of the survival of the fittest was said to justify racial hierarchies. Herbert Spencer wrote about how superior and muscular societies should not be held back by an interfering moralizing state. The science of eugenics—which appealed to many different streams of thought, even to a young social reformer, Tommy Douglas—justified the sterilization of the "unfit."

Only by understanding the depth and breadth of these ideas can we fully understand the enormity of what then happened and how a trio of policies emerged that wrought such havoc to human life and created the nightmare from which Aboriginal people are struggling to awaken. These policies were the passage of the Indian Act in 1876, the creation of compulsory residential schools, and the negotiation of treaties of which the purpose in the eyes of the settlers and their governments was to confine the Aboriginal people to small, remote communities or force those same people to lose their status if they left the reserve.

———

Aboriginal peoples in Ontario, Manitoba, Saskatchewan, Alberta, and parts of British Columbia live under treaties that were, for the most part, signed between the second half of the nineteenth century and the early twentieth century. We call these the "historic" treaties. The majority of Aboriginal people today are connected to land that is related to historic treaties.

These treaties were signed as the imperial Canadian state marched ever westward, clearing the way for a national railway and the economic development of the Prairies and beyond.

A relatively recent study on community well-being that looked at twenty-five years of data on outcomes in education, employment, income, and housing showed that between 1981 and 2006, modern treaty First Nations improved well-being at nearly twice the pace of historic treaty First Nations. Of all First Nations with treaties, Prairie First Nations had the lowest well-being scores.

There are a couple of ways to explain this growing inequality. The first is that the historic treaties were interpreted and administered by both federal and provincial governments as limiting Aboriginal people to reserves and giving up all traditional lands to the Crown. This view has never been accepted by the Aboriginal people, who have always insisted that they never abandoned jurisdiction and only agreed to share the land with newcomers and their governments. The other source of the divergence is forty years of progressive Supreme Court judgments and the related shifts in government policy toward the parts of Canada *without* historic treaties.

A lot of Canadian land is covered by these historic treaties, but not all. Much of the Yukon, the Northwest Territories, Quebec, British Columbia, and the entire eastern Arctic now known as Nunavut never had treaties that purported to address land. This is a major difference. And it has major consequences.

In 1973, shortly before I went to law school, the Supreme Court acknowledged in *Calder v. British Columbia* that Aboriginal people still had some rights ("Aboriginal title") to land that was not ceded to the Crown. A powerful dissent by Justices Hall, Spence, and Laskin in the case set out emphatically what many Canadians now realize to be true, namely that "the proposition . . . that after conquest or discovery the native people have no right at all except those subsequently granted or recognized by the conqueror or discoverer was wholly wrong." This changed everything, because before then governments had acted as if Aboriginal people had no land rights to areas they had traditionally occupied for hundreds or thousands of years.

In response to the *Calder* decision, there was a seismic shift in the federal government's approach. It had to acknowledge and deal with Aboriginal claims to land. All of a sudden,

Aboriginal groups had enormous leverage in negotiations over land and self-government. The era of comprehensive land claims began. This is why we have twenty-six modern treaties today and why more are on their way.

More Supreme Court decisions followed that further strengthened the hand of Aboriginal people with respect to their traditional lands. The *Delgamuukw* case in 1997 fleshed out the legal tests for proving Aboriginal title. And the *Tsilhqot'in* case of 2014 gave Aboriginal communities even more leverage.

All these Supreme Court decisions and policy changes were welcome and significant developments. But here's the thing: they had far less impact on lands covered by historic treaties. In those areas, the government considered the issue of land resolved. Ontario, Manitoba, Saskatchewan, and Alberta went on with business as usual. As a result, Aboriginal people in these provinces have been left with little power or capacity in their own homelands. They are consigned to tiny reserves. It is almost impossible for most people to make a decent living hunting, trapping, fishing, and gathering anymore, in large part because of widespread impact of industrial development projects. These First Nations are being denied their rightful share of revenue from major extraction projects in their traditional homelands. The fact is that with no land base and no revenue, these communities have limited futures apart from depending on the begging

Aboriginal people in these provinces have been left with little power or capacity in their own homelands.

bowl. Anyone who wants First Nations to be more prosperous and less dependent should be in favour of fundamental changes.

So we have this gap, and it is growing. We are leaving a huge number of Aboriginal people behind. It is impossible to justify the divergence between historic treaty areas and everywhere else. What's to be done about it?

The first step is to take a long hard look at the historic treaties, particularly at how they were negotiated and under what circumstances. And the closer one looks at the history, the uglier and more dubious these treaties look. There is a growing body of historical evidence that, in fact, some written treaties were forced on First Nations. They were, for the most part, take-it-or-leave-it documents signed under pressure by Aboriginal people with different languages and legal concepts, and there was never a common understanding about what they actually meant.

———

Two examples in particular show the true nature of the change wrought by the historic treaties: Treaty 6 and Treaty 9.

Treaty 6 covers a lot of the Prairies, including much of Saskatchewan. In 1878, the Conservative party under John A. Macdonald won the national election. The cornerstone of their platform was the construction of a railway to the Pacific Ocean. The trouble, of course, was that there were a lot of Aboriginal people already living on this land. The federal government wanted to build the national railway, the Canadian Pacific, as quickly as possible. To do that, it decided to get the

Indians out of the way by "clearing the plains," as the scholar James Daschuk has put it.

The government approached Aboriginal groups offering a treaty. Many were not interested. But the bargaining positions of the parties were hugely unequal. At the time, a famine had struck the Prairies. The bison, upon which Aboriginal people had relied for food and trade for thousands of years, had gone nearly extinct within a decade. Aboriginal people were dying of starvation en masse.

The federal government used the famine to strike a favourable deal for itself. It decided that it would withhold emergency food rations from communities that did not sign the treaty. A Liberal MP critic at the time, Malcolm Cameron, called this approach "a policy of submission shaped by a policy of starvation."

This was brutal, and it was effective. One after the next, Aboriginal leaders signed the treaty. One of them, Chief Thunderchild, promised that one day he would "retain a first-class lawyer." But he signed, and the government got what it wanted.

When our Supreme Court looks back at Canada's treaties with Aboriginal people, it calls them "solemn agreements." The Supreme Court tells us that the "honour of the Crown is always at stake" when dealing with Aboriginal people. It is always to be presumed that the government acts in good faith. The court says "sharp dealing" is not to be tolerated, now or in retrospect.

So what are we to make of Treaty 6? Was it honourable for the Crown to starve people into signing a treaty? Is it honourable for the Crown to enforce today a bad deal that it coerced people to sign over one hundred years ago? No. The answer is plainly no. If you put a gun to someone's head and force him to make a deal, this is not called a bargain. It is called robbery.

Treaty 9 covers the enormous expanse of Northern Ontario. In 1905, a group of treaty commissioners from Ottawa set off in canoes to get Aboriginal groups to sign a treaty. One of them was a man named Duncan Campbell Scott, who later became infamous as the architect of residential schools. Scott's motivation for the negotiations was quite simple: Canada needed this treaty to get access to, as he later put it, "many million feet of pulpwood, untold wealth of minerals, and un-harnessed waterpower sufficient to do the work of half the continent." The historical record makes clear that Canada wanted Aboriginal people to completely surrender their title to the land. But it is far from clear that this is what they agreed to.

Here's how negotiations for Treaty 9 worked: The terms of the treaty were predrafted, cooked up between Ottawa and Ontario. The commissioners could not alter them. The Aboriginal people approached to sign spoke limited or no English. They could not read the treaties they were asked to sign. Aboriginal leaders who signed the treaty could not write, so they were asked to put their hands on the top of pens as a government official signed an *X* for them.

What were these people told, in these very brief sessions along this canoe trip, to get them to mark that *X*? Today the terms of Treaty 9 govern the lives of about forty thousand Aboriginal people. There are very real, troubling, and unanswered questions about what was actually agreed upon.

There are two completely different narratives of what the historic treaties actually mean.

From the perspective of the government of Canada and of

provinces, what the treaties said was this: First Nations give up all claim to the land, surrender absolutely any claim to it, in exchange for which they would get, depending on the treaty, either four dollars or five dollars a year, the right to continue to live on a reserve, the right to continue to hunt on traditional territory, and some sense that they were being protected by the Crown. The treaties were set up to create the space for development, and the indigenous people must have known that when they signed.

The Aboriginal view was that the treaties were about sharing land, protection, and peace, as well as a promise of undiminished hunting and harvesting. Oral history as it has been passed down in Aboriginal communities does not conform to the Crown's view of treaties. There is also no evidence from notes taken by the commissioners or their staff that either the Aboriginals' surrender of the land or the restrictions on hunting and harvesting were ever discussed or explained.

In an article Duncan Campbell Scott published a year after the treaty was signed, he wrote this about the Indian understanding of the treaty negotiations: "What could they grasp of the pronouncement on the Indian tenure which had been delivered by the Law Lords of the Crown, what of the elaborate negotiations between the Dominion and the province which had made the treaty possible, what of the sense of traditional policy which brooded over the whole? Nothing. So there was no basis for argument."

When Scott says that "there was no basis for argument," we must then ask whether there was any basis for agreement at all. Or was the misunderstanding so fundamental as to make the treaty meaningless?

Today, looking back at historic treaties, there are a few ways they can be understood. Tom Flanagan, a long-time advisor to the Reform and Conservative parties, has said that "the deal is the deal." The wording of the treaties has to be seen as definitive. This is not simply his view but the argument that both the federal and provincial governments make in court. The trouble with this argument is its sheer implausibility.

The better option is to recognize that the deal, as interpreted by the Crown, is simply unfair. It is dishonourable to enforce agreements hastily discussed with people who could not read the language in which the terms of the treaty were written, people who received no legal advice or support even as they signed away almost all of their rights. In the case of Treaty 6, it was more than dishonourable to starve people into agreement. No one who takes a serious look at history can in good conscience support the Crown's current interpretation. It's ridiculous to think people would say, I have all this land, millions and millions and millions of acres of land, and I'm giving it to you for a few pieces of land that are five miles by five miles and a few dollars a year, and you promise to let me hunt and fish without interruption unless you decide otherwise, and to "take care of me." To put it in terms of a real estate transaction, it's preposterous. It doesn't make any sense.

This means we have to look carefully at the evidence that suggests that the treaty commissioners promised things orally that do not appear in the text. The Supreme Court has said that it is "unconscionable to ignore oral terms." We should take Aboriginal people seriously when they speak about what they really agreed to and what the treaties really mean. It will turn out that the real deal is a different deal. Only by having these discussions with Aboriginal people about the past can we have meaningful discourse with them in the present.

I am not someone who believes we should only rely on courts and judges to sort all these issues out. Much of the work must be done through negotiations and through politics. But the provincial governments of Alberta, Ontario, Saskatchewan, and Manitoba have shown little interest in revisiting the terms of the historic treaties, and neither has the federal government. This needs to change.

———

In the summer of 1992, all of the premiers agreed with the federal government that they would start self-government negotiations with First Nations. This became one of the key elements of the Charlottetown Accord that same year. We all know that this series of proposed amendments to the Constitution—including Senate reform—was defeated in a national referendum.

To put matters of dignity in blunt economic terms: healthier communities cost less to taxpayers.

But surely it can be argued that if self-government and new governance arrangements with all First Nations made sense to governments twenty-three years ago, it is about time we made progress today. The status quo is unacceptable, and it is costly. Whatever money the province may feel it is losing with revenue sharing will be more than paid off by the revitalization and empowerment of Aboriginal communities. To put matters of dignity in blunt economic terms: healthier communities cost less to taxpayers.

The historic treaties must be renewed and updated in line with the principle of sharing. There is a fear out there that renewing treaties means stopping economic development altogether. This fear is misplaced, a bogeyman that is actually the opposite of the truth. Conceding a fair share of the pie to First Nations will not mean an end to the feast. But it will mean a more equitable sharing of benefits. And without it, progress for everyone will be delayed.

We already have a model in the approach taken in Labrador. In this part of Canada, on land covered by a modern treaty with the Innu Nation, mining companies must reach mutually beneficial deals with the Innu. And in cases where the parties cannot come to an agreement on conditions for development, the matter is subject to compulsory arbitration. At the end of the day, a deal is always done. There is no reason we cannot take a similar approach in areas covered by historic treaties. As things stand today, the gap between people living under historic and modern treaties is widening. And it is unjustifiable.

> *The paternalism of the past, the remnants of colonialism that are still part of Canada's laws and bureaucratic structures need to go.*

The worse this gap gets, the more the governments of Canada, Ontario, Saskatchewan, Alberta, and Manitoba should be shamed into action. The status quo is certain to lead to more blockades and civil disobedience unless the provinces come to the table. Since the *Calder* case forty years ago, the courts have been delivering an unmistakable message: Settlers do not rule the land. They must share. And we are all here to stay. The process of accommodation, of negotiation, and of coming together must happen. It is the chapter in our national reconciliation that we must write together.

The paternalism of the past, the remnants of colonialism that are still part of Canada's laws and bureaucratic structures need to go. The model we have is broken. The federal department of Aboriginal affairs has to be taken apart, the Indian Act should be repealed, replaced by self-government agreements that go beyond the current reserve structure. This is an agenda that was set out years ago and has been sidelined by prevarication and a misplaced appeal to populism.

When high school dropout rates are what they are, when there is such a gap in health, in income, in life expectancy, in housing, in economic development, we need the courage to say the current model is broken and needs to be fixed.

When young girls and boys are taking their lives because they see no hope it is not just an issue of jobs and governance. It is a deep crisis of the spirit. It is a cry of the heart and the soul. None of us can be indifferent to that cry, none of us can turn away from the abuse and addiction that have been allowed to swallow up too many.

The need for recognition, for change, is the human rights challenge of our time in Canada. There was a

> *The need for recognition, for change, is the human rights challenge of our time in Canada.*

time when many Canadians could turn away from these issues because they were far away, away from the centres of population, away from awareness. This is no longer true. The great movement from reserve to city is well under way—what was "out there" is now "in here," and the issues and challenges have to be dealt with and faced head-on.

———

When Chief Justice Marshall of the U.S. Supreme Court presided over a majority decision that insisted that only the national government could make decisions on Indian affairs, President Andrew Jackson famously remarked, "John Marshall has made his decision; now let him enforce it. . . . Build a fire under them. When it gets hot enough, they'll go." And that's exactly what happened as the Cherokee Nation, like the Choctaws and Seminoles before them, were forcibly removed from their homes and driven down what became known as the Trail of Tears to Indian Territory.

It is a truly shameful episode in modern history, but it is Andrew Jackson's comment that drives home the dilemma that is faced even today. Since the early 1970s the First Nations, Inuit, and Métis people have been winning substantial and important legal battles. What is deeply troubling is the gap between the court decisions and the willingness of both provincial and federal governments to enforce and follow those decisions.

As Murray Sinclair, the chairman of the Truth and Reconciliation Commission, put it so succinctly when he quoted the aphorism, "The truth will set you free, but first it will piss you off."

The dilemma remains that the majority of Canadians, and the parties that strive to represent them in Parliament, think about these issues as little as they have to. They will not be front and centre in any election campaign, and these relationships are as subject to misunderstanding, stereotype, and sheer ignorance as any public policy in the country.

The reason for the lack of leadership is not hard to figure out—it has everything to do with a read of public opinion itself. A majority of Canadians do not see these issues as a priority.

But the issues will not go away or get any easier as time goes on. As mentioned, the indigenous population is the fastest growing in the country, and it will become an increasing factor in the urban communities where most Canadians live. And resource development is now extending deep into the traditional territory of people who have strong views about their own jurisdiction, rights, and needs. Governments and companies ignore these realities at their peril.

Some governments and premiers understand this, and some not so much. But if the insistence of our constitutional law that accommodations must be reached is not matched by serious political action, the result will not be a trail of tears. It will be a series of confrontations, large and small, that in themselves will require a response. The purely majoritarian theory of democracy is not good enough. A richer view of constitutional democracy is required. But that in itself is a challenge, to which I now turn.

CHAPTER FIVE

WHAT'S HAPPENED TO DEMOCRACY IN CANADA?

W e live in a constitutional democracy, which means a form of government controlled by the people in which the exercise of power is limited and constrained by the rule of law. The phrase "rule of law" is a term widely used to mean not just the rule of laws but the rule of justice. This is not merely a definitional point or a legal quibble. All regimes in the world operate by the rule of laws—Nazi Germany had an elaborate legal structure, and we know from a remarkable body of scholarship that even that most brutal of decisions, the one that was taken at Wannsee in January 1942 to establish an industry of death and complete the total destruction of the Jewish people, was made in a fully documented way and governed by a set of systematic rules.

What distinguishes the rule of justice from the simple rule of laws is the acceptance that there are basic principles that extend beyond mere politics. In Canada and other Western countries, we share certain values about society that have found their way into principles, and constitutional documents, that are designed to limit the exercise of power and to ensure individual freedom.

It is also about respecting that the power of the people is limited by what's fair to minorities, what's reasonable, and by what's legal and constitutional.

Perhaps the most famous of these in the British constitutional tradition, of which Canada is a part, is the Magna Carta, "the great charter." Signed by King John in Runnymede, England, in 1215, the document stated that the monarch's power could only be exercised in a certain way and that the nobles around him could not have their property and lives destroyed on the whim of a royal signature.

Constitutional democracy always has to be distinguished not just from tyranny and dictatorship but as well from populist democracy, which would mean a rule by public opinion unencumbered by the rule of justice. This points to a central tension in our very idea and practice of democracy—it is not a simple appeal to the rule of the majority. It is also about respecting that the power of the people is limited by what's fair to minorities, what's reasonable, and by what's legal and constitutional.

Debate and disagreement are necessary aspects of this

reconciliation between the rule of the majority and the rule of law. That two people—or two parties—might differ on an issue is not a reason to shut down the conversation. It is a sign of a healthy democracy. The discussion over the niqab and whether it can be worn in a citizenship swearing-in is an example of one such area where Canadians are navigating the grey area where political and legal jurisdiction overlap. Questions of digital privacy and security are another. In all such cases, citizens will only feel enfranchised and that their democratic institutions affect them when the laws of their democracy accurately reflect and uphold their belief system.

From 1867 to the patriation of the Constitution in 1982, the primary limit to the power of one government or another was the federal nature of the country. The provinces and the federal government spent a lot of time going to court—first to the Privy Council in London and then to the Supreme Court of Canada—arguing about which government had the power to do what. Federalism by its very nature is an important limit on the power of government because it insists that power be defined and that it be shared. Understanding the federal nature of Canada has always been a hallmark of Canadian statecraft. What Jacques

Federalism by its very nature is an important limit on the power of government because it insists that power be defined and that it be shared.

Parizeau once called "endless trips to the dentist" is in fact a critical feature of adult political life in Canada—accepting that each level of government has a job to do but that they are neighbours and that their interests and concerns are important too. Negotiation in this sense is not a chore or a pain but a necessary feature of a world in which you don't want the most powerful or the most insistent to always get their way. And, by the way, going to the dentist is what you do when you want to avoid further pain.

In the discussion of power sharing among levels of government, we must not forget to include municipalities. For all Canadians, the places where most of us live, our cities, still lack the powers and capacity to respond to our needs. Governments that are farther away, in provincial capitals and in Ottawa, hold most of the taxing power and most of the purse strings. From Victoria to St. John's, mayors and councils are left to wrestle with unacceptable choices because they simply don't have the means to get to a better place. Governments must serve their citizens, so when city councils, whose decisions most immediately impact Canadians, find their hands tied, the everyday lives of Canadians suffer. The result does nothing to convince citizens of the efficacy of responsible federalism.

It is a myth that the Charter is a centralizing document. Canada today is the most decentralized federation in the world, and the Charter does not give any additional powers to the federal government. Rather, it limits the powers of all governments. This has been reaffirmed time and again by the Supreme Court of Canada in countless cases since 1982. If Parliament or provincial legislatures aren't prepared to recognize individual rights, the courts will step in, not in the name of either level of government, but in the name of freedom and democracy.

———

If our Constitution remains a subject of continuing debate, then the same is equally true of Canadian criminal law. This has been an area of controversy for centuries, and it reflects the tension in our values and culture about the nature of criminality and the purposes of punishment. In each generation, the issue is resolutely alive. In modern times, reformers as far back as the Italian criminologist Cesare Beccaria in the eighteenth century and the British philosopher Jeremy Bentham in the nineteenth focused their arguments on the need for punishment to be suited to each crime and for said punishment to be effective in reducing crime and in helping the criminal to reform and recover. The protection of society remains pre-eminent, but the means of achieving this protection should be constantly judged according to the evidence. What works becomes the basic test, and it can change over time.

In contrast, we have the view held by a great many that the denunciation of crime is a role of both law and corrections. This view holds that the moral fabric of society is offended and threatened by criminality and that the purpose of the law is to reaffirm our common sense of outrage at crimes against the person and property. This view is strengthened by what is seen as a deep sense of insecurity in the broader society created by violent crime and violent criminals. Only harsher and more certain punishment will assuage public opinion and satisfy the need for moral denunciation.

The difference between these two views is not simply an academic difference between two philosophies. Conservative political parties have consistently used the second approach to distinguish between those who are tough on crime and those who are not. Some have pandered to public stereotypes as to who criminals are, and they have not been afraid to play the race card. "Criminals" becomes a euphemism for "blacks," or "Aboriginals," and the makeup of the prison population reflects the view that the more these groups are kept behind bars the safer the rest of the population will be. In Canada, we are confronted with specific questions about crime, restorative justice, and race that we should be looking to. How can we simplify and rationalize our criminal laws? How can we divert people from jail rather than thrust them into it? And how can we be as tough with the causes of crime as with crime itself?

It is a great irony that those who praise freedom as the ultimate human value and want to see a steady reduction in the size of the state in the economic sphere have been busy turning two major expressions of Canadian law—the Income Tax Act and the Criminal Code—into documents of truly biblical proportions. These texts are fatter and more detailed than ever before, with more loopholes in the former and proscriptions in the latter, and they leave any successor governments with deep challenges.

In an article on the website FiveThirtyEight, Oliver Roeder reported on a recent study by the Brennan Center for Justice in the United States. The study pointed out that the prison population in the United States has exploded, with over 4 million Americans currently behind bars. With around 5 percent of the world's population, America has fully 25 percent of the world's prisoners. The costs of this incarceration are proving prohibitive, with some states spending as much on prisons as they do on public universities, and even American conservatives are becoming convinced that the war on crime and the war on drugs have proven to be disastrous, and expensive, failures.

As compelling as this argument might seem, it does little to persuade those who are convinced that the purpose of criminal justice is to uphold a moral order. We face major challenges in Canada with rates of incarceration among First Nations and indigenous people rising well in excess of population numbers. Again, conservatives contend that this is not an indication of discrimination but rather a reflection of the extent of gang and criminal behavior in the urban core of many cities. As these arguments persist and the stream of at-risk individuals sent to jail continues, unre-

Demography has more to do with criminality than anything else, and excessive incarceration can even become a source of higher crime rates.

lenting, politicians and lawyers persist in talking past one another and ignoring the broader implications.

This is not about leniency or softheadedness. Quite the contrary. It's about understanding that demography has more to do with criminality than anything else, and that excessive incarceration can even become a source of higher crime rates. A generation of young men, and increasingly women, left without work or dignity will turn to crime if there are no alternatives. And so we can only hope that the Supreme Court will continue to insist that the punishment has to fit the crime in each individual case.

No individual has been a stronger exponent of the importance of the independence of the judiciary and the constitutional role of the Supreme Court in a democracy than Chief Justice Beverley McLachlin. The chief justice has been a judge since 1980, and she has served on the Supreme Court of Canada since 1989, culminating in her appointment as chief justice in 2000. Virtually her entire judicial career has been spent in the era of the Charter. Her defence of the Charter on criminal law and personal liberty issues has been forthright, and she has done a remarkable job in bringing the court to strong consensus judgments on difficult issues like Aboriginal rights and assisted suicide.

Chief Justice McLachlin's defence of the court's role has been rightly unapologetic. In adopting the Charter, and in asserting in section 35 that existing Aboriginal and treaty rights were affirmed in the act of patriation, Parliament was extending the rule of law and limiting its own unlimited jurisdiction. As opposed to the British model, the Constitution, and not Parliament alone, represented Canadian law and sovereignty. As I showed previously, we would not have made much progress on Aboriginal issues as a country in the last thirty years without the Charter, section 35, and the court. Majorities left to their own devices will often ignore and suppress minorities.

But any court is only as good as its appointees, and it must be said that the Supreme Court of Canada, led by Chief Justice McLachlin, has done a remarkable job. The court has taken the entrenchment of the Charter to mean that Parliament must have been serious when it affirmed that certain procedural rights embedded in our justice system were fundamental and needed to be protected. This has meant that courts have questioned the insistence that minimum standards of sentencing should be set by statute and not by judicial discretion.

Crime rates are falling, yet the numbers in jail are growing. Political parties are not asking the right questions. They are not questioning whether the policy is effective but instead concern themselves with whether it meets two quite different tests—political support and satisfying the need for moral denunciation. Evidence does

Crime rates are falling, yet the numbers in jail are growing.

not fit into the equation. But in reality, a departure from evidence means that money is wasted, lives are thrown away, and we are no safer, freer, or more secure as a result.

The pursuit of populism at the expense of the rule of law does not end with the criminal law. It affects the way in which Parliament itself is portrayed and described to Canadians. Not too subtly, Canadians are being told that elections are about choosing a prime minister, when in fact it's about choosing Parliament. This parallels the way in which power in our system is increasingly centralized and revolves around the personality and control of the first minister.

In a parliamentary system, elections produce a parliament, and that parliament makes a government. Prattle about "winning a mandate" with less than a majority in Parliament is just that—partisan spin, all sound and fury, signifying nothing. It is a lesson worth remembering.

Even without proportional representation, Canada's three-party system will often produce a minority result in an election, and it seems passing strange that we would not even admit the possibility that dialogue and negotiation should follow from an election and that agreements on how to ensure parliamentary accountability, respect for the electoral result, and more efficient and less anarchic ways to govern in minority Parliaments (by ensuring few votes are actually confidence measures) are better than bravado, intimidation, and revolving door elections.

Prattle about "winning a mandate" with less than a majority in Parliament is just that—partisan spin, all sound and fury, signifying nothing.

Recent history shows the merits of this thinking. Heading into my first Ontario provincial election after leaving Ottawa for Queen's Park, I spent some time reflecting on the probability of a minority result in the three-way competition that had emerged in Ontario in the 1970s. There had already been two minority governments in 1975 and 1977, and in each instance the Tories, led by Bill Davis, had effectively played the NDP and the Liberals against each other, eventually steering their way through to a majority in 1981. Pierre Trudeau had employed the same strategy in the 1972 to 1974 period.

In the election of 1985, my first as NDP provincial leader, Miller's Conservatives won fifty-two seats with about 37 percent of the vote, Peterson and the Liberals won forty-eight seats with roughly the same percentage of votes, and the NDP won twenty-five seats with about 24 percent of the vote. On the night of the election, the commentators went to bed thinking that the Conservatives had secured a minority. The media declared Frank Miller the winner—despite his having failed to win a majority—and the Conservatives were confident that they had a right to govern, as they had been doing for forty-two years.

But I was not convinced that politics could just go on as before, and a few days later, I called David Peterson, then the Liberal party leader, and we discussed doing something different. Rather than allow our two parties to be played off of each other, as had happened for years prior, we considered what might be gained if we were to instead work side by side.

Some voices within my party at the time were dead set against any coalition, be it with the Liberals or the Conservatives. The NDP would lose its purity and its principles, the argument went, and would do better to vote on a case-by-case basis in the House, leaving the Tories to govern. Others argued that such a move was not legal or constitutional. But expert voices, such as Eugene Forsey—who at that time was generally recognized as a constitutional guru—agreed that an arrangement between two parties, each with fewer seats than the governing party but able together to command a working majority in the House, was "constitutional in every respect" and insisted that we had the obligation to explore every option to create a stable and working legislature.

The majority view that emerged was that a public agreement between the NDP and the Liberals, based on clear objectives and timelines, would be a better option than the Russian roulette of a minority government living by its wits day by day. My own sense was that we had to decontaminate the notion of a minority Parliament being synonymous with instability and show people that the legislature could work better.

The accord that was negotiated was not a coalition but a working partnership. The joint Liberal and NDP government gave up the right to declare votes of confidence whenever it wanted, limiting itself to budget bills. It would accept a loss on anything else. The deal would last for two years, and the government committed itself to a series of measures—on pay equity, labour law reform, social housing, environmental legislation, the protection of Medicare, and many others, all pursued within a framework of fiscal responsibility—with timelines clearly set out. A management committee of both parties would meet regularly to monitor the progress of the agreement.

Despite these discussions, the Conservatives still insisted on meeting the House and bringing in a Throne Speech. But their defeat followed soon after, and a new government was sworn in without a constitutional crisis. The accord government worked effectively and efficiently, and it passed the laws it said it would.

The point of this story is simply this: a minority Parliament does not have to be unstable. A government has to command the support of the legislature. And surrounding it all has to be a conversation about how to make government and Parliament work.

But instead of showing this effort to cooperate or negotiate according to Canadian parliamentary law and tradition, recent governments have turned Canada's Constitution on its head, certainly pointing south. Elections are becoming essentially a presidential affair, with the prime ministership automatically going to the leader with the most seats. We must remember that it is members of Parliament who are elected, and ultimately the prime ministership (or premiership) depends on who can command a majority in Parliament.

The effort to make Canadians ignore the foundation of the parliamentary system—that the leader of the party able to command a majority in the House of Commons becomes prime minister—is only one part of how Parliament is being ignored. One hundred and fifty years ago, the British commentator Walter Bagehot described how politics in Britain really worked. There was a difference between the real and ceremonial aspects of the system. Parliament limited the power of the monarchy, but Bagehot also noted that parliamentary power itself was increasingly dominated by the cabinet. Modern-day observers of the parliamentary system have noted that this has now evolved still further, as more power is concentrated in the hands of the prime minister and his own staff and bureaucracy.

Voters rightly feel that there's something wrong with how our democracy is working—or, more accurately, how it isn't. We don't yet have the deadlock of the United States, but we do have another kind of deadlock—the hard hand of too much party discipline and too much power in the hands of the prime minister. Some commentators have made this a personal attack on Stephen Harper, but the reality is that the underlying trend both precedes Mr. Harper and is increasingly common in the other parties as well.

An excessive partisanship is what Canadians see. And they don't like it. Nor are MPs happy to be treated like cannon fodder. Parliament should be the place where real debate and give-and-take happens. Alas, it is not.

Doing politics differently means changing the way Parliament works to ensure a more democratic Canada. From Question Period (where everyone is rigidly choreographed) to committees (where little real exchange happens and the wills of the whips prevail) it is past time for a change.

An excessive partisanship is what Canadians see. And they don't like it.

Caucus discipline need not apply to every vote, and every measure before the House should not be a matter of confidence. I say let the caucus be more raucous. And let the House of Commons do its job in a way that respects individual members. Let committees work freely, setting their own agendas and electing their own chairs. Let them study the subject matter of bills before they come to the House. Committees in which there is genuine give-and-take and real responsibility will become surprisingly productive and less partisan. Members will stop screaming at one another when they realize they have something to learn from one another and that they will be held accountable for their decisions.

In the late eighteenth century, the British Parliament debated a famous resolution, worded simply as follows: "That the powers of the King are increasing, and ought to be reduced." Since the time of the Glorious Revolution a hundred years before, Britain's Parliament had been seized with a major issue: the powers of the monarch were growing with patronage and a corrupt electoral system.

The issue before our Parliament today is remarkably similar. The prime minister appoints a cabinet, caucus chairs, and hundreds of public service jobs. Whether from the governor general or officers of Parliament, there are few limits or checks to his choices. Business leaders worry about raising a voice for fear of reprisal. Local media that are out of line get punished.

The proclivity for omnibus bills is yet another example of what is wrong with Parliament. A 2012 budget bill changed seventy laws, gutted environmental protection, killed off a multitude of agencies, and raised the age of retirement from sixty-five to sixty-seven. Shortly after introducing the bill, the government limited debate, and this massive, four-hundred-page monstrosity headed to committee for a pro forma discussion. The speed with which this sweeping legislation was shepherded through a supposedly open democratic process should have every Canadian—whether he or she agrees with the contents of the bill or not—outraged.

The only thing that can change this over time is the election of a government that seriously commits to limiting the power of the prime minister and that agrees to sharing power with Parliament and the people. Canada's political parties spend a few years in opposition and then govern as if it's permanent payback time. All three parties have everything to play for, and Canadians are deeply dissatisfied, rightly so, with how Parliament is failing. But the parties are all afraid of addressing any issue that might tie their hands when they're in government.

We're now living in a democracy with dictatorial tendencies, and Canadians should not see their democratic institutions diluted and muzzled because of political timidity. Are Canadians ready to make a change?

If the House of Commons badly needs reforming, the same could be said in spades about the second chamber, the Senate. When the Fathers of Confederation met to decide on what kind of second chamber we needed, there weren't any truly democratic models to choose from. The House of Lords was a hereditary body with a smattering of newly minted earls or dukes to add to the mix. American senators were, at the time of confederation, chosen by the state legislators. In a decision that very much reflected Sir John A.'s view that the federation needed a central government whose seniority and control of the country's direction could not easily be challenged, senators were to be men (of course), property holders, people of means, and loyal to the prime minister and political party that appointed them.

If the House of Commons badly needs reforming, the same could be said in spades about the second chamber, the Senate.

If it had been up to the Supreme Court of Canada in the 1920s, the Senate would have remained a men's club. It took an appeal to the Privy Council in London to save the cause of gender equality in Senate appointments. Women were not persons in 1867, but the Law Lords wisely found a way for them to reach that exalted status in 1929.

Various efforts have been made over the years to reform the Senate, to make it elected, to bring its membership closer in line with provincial preferences. Starting in the 1970s, a movement based in western Canada called for a "Triple E Senate": equal between provinces, elected, and effective. Triple E became an article of faith for the Reform Party. Ironically, the closest the country came to adopting this kind of reform was in the Charlottetown Accord, which the Reform Party actively opposed in the 1992 national referendum.

When Stephen Harper won government in 2006, he promised Senate reform, including term limits and, most important, a commitment to appoint senators who had been elected in a provincially sanctioned process. Insisting that he still believed in a Triple E Senate, Mr. Harper realized that this would require a constitutional amendment, but he was loath to take that path. He believed that he could institute an elected Senate by stealth, after which—once the elected senators became more numerous—the pressure for equality and effectiveness would grow. Mr. Harper's problem was that while stealth might work, subterfuge would not. After much delay, he finally acknowledged that a reference to the Supreme Court would be required. Quebec had already started the process, though, so his hand was forced, and it was left to the Supreme Court, in a unanimous opinion, to remind Mr. Harper and his government of the ABCs of constitutional government.

The court's decision was clear. Canada is a federation, a constitutional government in which the power of both the federal and provincial governments is defined and limited. The makeup, appointment process, and powers of the Senate are clearly set out in the Constitution. An institution so fundamental cannot be changed, or done away with, by Parliament acting alone. To change its method of selection, and the terms of its members, will require the support of Parliament plus seven provincial legislatures whose populations make up more than half that of Canada. To abolish the Senate will require unanimity.

Those who oppose the ruling say that the court has endorsed the status quo and that changing the Senate is now impossible. This is another act of spin. The court has no opinion about the Senate, its utility, or its value. It neither praises nor condemns the institution. It simply tells us all to give our heads a shake and understand the Constitution of Canada. Senate reform, and other constitutional change, can happen if there is enough strong desire for it to happen. It means the federal and provincial governments would have to start talking to one another and that someone would have to exercise leadership. To say this is impossible is to take our current lethargy, backbiting, and political churlishness as normal for all time.

A prime minister could always make better appointments to the Senate. He could make it a place where contrary opinions are welcome. He could, by these appointments, encourage it to be less partisan and more thoughtful. And he could, slowly, quietly, encourage backchannel conversations about how to make constitutional change possible. If most provinces insist on referenda to approve change, it's fair to say it becomes that much harder to do. But never say never.

Should constitutional change be a top priority, a make or break, for any government? No, that would be unwise. But neither should we walk around blaming the court for our problems. More often than not, we are the authors of our own misfortune. The silver lining is that changing the situation is also within our control.

———————

It has often been said that those not prepared to learn from history are doomed to repeat it. One thing we know for certain is that the character of a country's democracy has to reflect its history, its people, its texture. We forget now the fallout from the failure to complete the ratification of the Meech Lake Accord. As a result of that failure, support for Quebec independence jumped twenty-five points in the polls, and yet the next round of constitutional discussion couldn't just be about Quebec. The decision to broaden the discussion, and the table, in subsequent talks in Charlottetown meant that the more inclusive process was messy, confused, hard to manage. And yet it responded to very real demands to be part of the process.

The end result was an agreement reached by First Ministers and Aboriginal leaders in Charlottetown in late August 1992 — it recognized Quebec's distinctiveness, created an elected and equal Senate with a way to break a deadlock with the House of Commons, ensured a stronger social and economic union in the country while allowing for greater flexibility, and entrenched Aboriginal self-government with a timetable for negotiations. A short few weeks later, though, the accord was defeated in a referendum, and Mr. Chrétien promised when he was elected a year later that he would not mention the word "constitution."

No doubt Charlottetown had its flaws. The process of ratification was rushed. The country was surprised by the breadth and extent of it. There were too many targets for those who wanted to stop it. But it's hard to say that this new approach of pretending there are no problems is the answer either. The issues raised twenty years ago are with us today, but we've lost the habit of a national conversation. And that's not good; in fact, it's dangerous.

It will take a new government to share a vision about the future and discuss it with Canadians, with premiers, with Aboriginal leaders. All Canadians need inspiration about who we are and where we're going. Canada is one of those countries whose very existence can never be taken for granted. Prompted in part while I read Chantal Hébert and Jean Lapierre's book *The Morning After*, a series of interviews with the major actors involved in the Quebec referendum of 1995, I was struck by the realization that there were deep anxieties and divisions on all sides and that in the face of rapidly changing scenarios, the uncertainty as to what could or should have happened was overwhelming.

> *All Canadians need inspiration about who we are and where we're going.*

How political leaders react when they appear to be ten points ahead in the polls is completely different from when momentum has suddenly shifted. Mr. Chrétien, who had dismissed constitutional preoccupations when he became prime minister, was suddenly forced to declare in his final speech in Verdun that powers would be shifted to the provinces and Quebec would be recognized as a distinct society. He was on the edge, and he knew it.

This is not just an issue that arises in the midst of a national crisis. The desire for governments and politics to connect more personally to the condition of the people is not an abstraction. The emergence of institutions and bureaucracies that transcend nation-states is the story of modern Europe, and it is now a deeply contested story. The economic crisis of 2008–09 laid bare the fragility of many countries' finances, as well as the enormous difficulty of managing economies without also being able to manage currencies. The euro seemed a noble idea, but its problem was that it stretched across national frontiers and governments whose people had entirely different expectations. Financial prudence for some became a stranglehold for others, and finding the right balance has proved more than just difficult, it has been at times virtually impossible.

And, as we know only too well from modern history, economies and governments that are unable to deliver the goods, to provide the basic necessities of life to their people, then become prey to their worst instincts and reactions. Anti-immigrant, anti-Semitic, anti-everything—movements that seemed inconceivable a generation ago suddenly break down all barriers between left and right, between progressive and reactionary.

Democracy, then, is challenged in Canada, as it is everywhere in the world. The key political and legal institutions—the courts, the House of Commons, and the Senate—all have their role to play, but citizens feel a growing frustration with

The growing disaffection with politics in democratic countries is no longer a passing trend. The consequences of the phenomenon will become even more severe with the passage of time.

how our concerns are brought to bear. As a result, many question the institutions themselves. A healthy citizenry requires a healthy democracy. Unless we ensure that our democratic institutions and processes are transparent, well managed, and clearly defined across all levels of government, we cannot guarantee their longevity. The growing disaffection with politics in democratic countries is no longer a passing trend. The consequences of the phenomenon will become even more severe with the passage of time. This internal political estrangement is something we must address as a country to ensure that Canada remains truly free for future generations.

CHAPTER SIX

WHAT'S HAPPENED TO CANADA IN THE WORLD?

While my father Saul was Canadian ambassador to the United Nations from 1972 to 1976, he served at the same time as Daniel Patrick Moynihan, who came to the United Nations as American ambassador with a mission to use that job as a stepping-stone to the Senate. Moynihan gave many speeches denouncing the United Nations as a den of gross injustice and hypocrisy, and he wanted above all to use his command of the microphone as a kind of bully pulpit from which to lecture the rest of the world.

In his memoir of those years, Moynihan singled out my father as one of those diplomats who was always looking for compromise and who was less than enthusiastic about Moynihan's assault on the United Nations and all its evils.

In a memo that he wrote to Ottawa at the time, my dad made it clear that his differences with Moynihan were not simply ones of temperament. My father showed audacity, disagreeing profoundly with the strategy of megaphone diplomacy, of failing to understand that the world was made up of many governments and regimes that did bad things, and that simply denouncing them, and the United Nations, as a forum of iniquity was counterproductive. In my dad's view, such posturing was not the way to produce desired results—it did, however, get Ambassador Moynihan his seat in the U.S. Senate.

The United Nations is really just a reflection of the world of extremes and irrationalities in which we have always lived. Navigating the many concerns and issues that confront its assembly is difficult, but "stop the world, I want to get off" is never a sensible strategy. It has rightly been said that courage is the most important virtue because it is the one that makes all the others possible. The same can be said for its closely related cousins, resilience and persistence. Such qualities have been a part of Canada, its service to the world, and its history since well before my father's time.

In recent years, Canada has become the classic practitioner of megaphone diplomacy, the place where playing to the domestic gallery trumps what we do in the rest of the world. We lecture everyone, close embassies for symbolic reasons, and generally position ourselves as it suits a domestic audience that has already been carved into a thousand slices to consume the latest home-delivered message. Such diplomacy is called principled, but that confuses noise with effectiveness.

Imagine a different approach. Imagine, for example, if a

few years ago we had kept our small embassy in Tehran open, with a seasoned diplomat and a couple of bright political and legal officers. Imagine if they had kept open a window for potential change, as we did for years in Moscow at the height of the Cold War.

Imagine if we had diplomats who were allowed to explain to Canadians what is happening. And imagine if the prime minister was inclined to pick up the phone and ask for their opinion and advice. Imagine if our political intelligence on foreign states allowed us to separate the rhetoric from the reality, to understand the differences in governance, or to take a leading role in international affairs.

As a country that is less than a superpower, Canada cannot rely on its muscle to make itself heard. Our influence comes from a capacity for wisdom, from being a trusted source of information, knowledge, and judgment on some of the most difficult issues facing the world.

Instead, Canada has become a posturer, a poseur, a political game player. Canada has become a right-wing gasbag, shouting from the sidelines. It was not always this way, and it does not have to be this way in the future. We would do well to remember a different kind of Canada and a better approach to diplomacy and politics. Our past was not perfect, but it was better than what

Imagine if we had diplomats who were allowed to explain to Canadians what is happening. And imagine if the prime minister was inclined to pick up the phone and ask for their opinion and advice.

we've seen in recent times. It is only natural that our foreign policy should reflect both our interests and our values. Canada's role on the global stage could be that of a valued source of reasoned, thoughtful advice to powers afraid or unwilling to talk to one another, clear minded about the current risks and dangers in the world, prepared to speak up and speak out but also willing to engage and to listen. The debate as to whether what we do in the world should be realistic or idealistic is pretty empty.

———

Coming to terms with the world around us, understanding and learning about it, is how we learn and grow as people. It is also how we learn and grow as a country. Canada is a nation of 35 million people, with an advanced economy and sovereignty over vast lands on the northern half of the North American continent. Well over half our national income depends on trade outside our borders, most of it with the United States, but much of which is increasingly connected to a world whose growth has many different centres around the globe.

> *Canada's role on the global stage could be that of a valued source of reasoned, thoughtful advice to powers afraid or unwilling to talk to one another, clear minded about the current risks and dangers in the world.*

We value freedom and the rule of law, for ourselves and for others. As we have seen, we're an Aboriginal country as well as a country of immigrants and settlers. This Aboriginal-settler dynamic will be reflected in how we connect with countries and communities with similar issues. From the Americas to Australia to Russia and the Nordic countries, questions of human rights, economics and community development, and cultural integrity are part of a shared experience. It is only natural that the Inuit people of the far north want a deep connection with other peoples in the polar communities. Our sensitivity and understanding of issues of climate change, cultural and educational challenges, and resource development should reflect this part of the Canadian reality. We need to embrace this aspect of our personality and recognize it as part of who we are.

When Canada became a federal, self-governing country in 1867, our foreign policy was run by the British. Border disputes with the Americans, arguments about trade, and our foreign obligations were all handled for us by the British, sometimes to our detriment. The completely illogical border between Canada and Alaska owes everything to our colonial status at the time. No Canadian government could have survived such an embarrassment if the decision had been ours to make.

The federal cabinet that declared war in 1914 was presided over by the governor general, a British duke. But as young Canadian boys died in droves on the battlefields of northern France, our identity came to the fore. It is often said that this identity owes much to the sacrifices and victories at places like Vimy Ridge, but it's also true that it was Robert Borden's insistence that the costs of war should give us more say in the construction of a postwar world. So it was that Canada joined the League of Nations in 1919 as an independent country. We shared the hardships of the world depression in the '30s, and like many others, we were fooled into thinking that reason would work its charm on Hitler.

We fought on the battlefields again and assumed our place at the United Nations in the years after the Second World War. We are a founder of NATO and had much to do with writing its charter. A Canadian, John Humphrey, was a drafter of the Universal Declaration of Human Rights. In the aftermath of the destruction of Europe in 1945, we quickly became natural, nimble, and effective internationalists.

Canada's rise as a middle power and influential diplomatic player is best symbolized by a historic vote at the U.N. General Assembly on November 7, 1956. On that day, the United Nations decided to create an emergency force to supervise the withdrawal of Israeli, British, and French troops from Egyptian territory around the Suez Canal and to ensure the maintenance of a cease-fire agreement that would last for eleven years. The United Nations Emergency Force (UNEF), as it was called, soon became known as "the blue berets"—soldiers working under the flag not of their own country, but under that of the United Nations itself.

The Canadian diplomat and politician front and centre on this day in New York was Lester Pearson, a man whose intelligence, charm, and personal skills put together a resolution to this Suez conflict, which was threatening the peace of the region and the world. As Pearson told the General Assembly, "We need action not only to end the fighting but to make the peace" (November 2, 1956). His personal contribution would receive its due recognition when Pearson won the Nobel Peace Prize in 1957, the first and only Canadian to be personally recognized in this way.

One man whose role in the response to the Suez invasion has been underrated is Louis St. Laurent, the Canadian prime minister. He was outraged at what he saw as an act of deep folly and illegality, and he encouraged Pearson to do everything possible to avert a deeper crisis. Pearson, then Canada's foreign minister, was uniquely placed to do just that. Widely respected in Washington and London, he was equally well known in the corridors of the United Nations. He had been elected president of the General Assembly in 1952, and his breezy and avuncular style made him well liked among delegations from many countries. His own personal experiences in the First World War had forged a deep opposition to armed conflict, and this was re-enforced by his diplomatic work in the second great conflict. He was ably assisted by a group of young Canadians who themselves were present at the creation of the new world order after 1945 and saw the Department of External Affairs as the best place to express their commitment to a world governed by rules.

In his famous speech in Fulton, Missouri, in 1946, Winston Churchill emphasized that in order to police the conflicts that would inevitably emerge in the years ahead, the United Nations itself needed a fighting force, stating that "courts and magistrates may be set up but they cannot function without sheriffs and constables." The Korean conflict had seen the United Nations directly involved in defence of the sovereignty of South Korea. Pearson shrewdly saw the idea of a peacekeeping force as accomplishing two objectives—building the credibility of the United Nations and getting the Suez invaders off the hook.

And so the baby was born, the subject of many compromises

and redrafts, imperfect but still a proud moment for Lester Pearson and for Canada. When the General Assembly passed the resolution that established the U.N. Emergency Force on November 7, 1956, the delegates surrounded the Canadian desk in the forum, offering congratulations to Pearson and his team. Canada has been at the centre of the action: constructive, engaged, and effective.

Lest it be thought that only Liberals contributed to this sense of Canada, John Diefenbaker and Brian Mulroney played their part as well. Diefenbaker did not need Harold Macmillan to tell him that the "wind of change" was blowing through Africa and that apartheid was a regime on the losing end of history. He saw the importance of deeper alliances with India and the newly independent countries of Africa, and he led the way to the exclusion of South Africa from the Commonwealth. It is worth noting, though, that Diefenbaker did not cut off diplomatic ties with South Africa despite his deep-seated opposition to the racist regime.

Brian Mulroney's leadership within the Commonwealth on the South Africa file was equally forthright. He argued for stronger sanctions and used Canada's strong networks in Africa and among church organizations to build a powerful case for change. When Nelson Mandela was finally released from his decades-long stay in prison and came to Canada in the spring of 1990, he made it a point, publicly and in private, to emphasize what Canada and Mulroney personally had done to make his liberation and political success a reality.

Jean Chrétien's wise decision not to support the invasion of Iraq was not taken after reading a poll. It was taken because of the Canadian government's principled view that the invasion was illegal and its pragmatic concern that an invasion can very quickly become an unpopular occupation. He was right. His government also made great efforts to extend the rule of law internationally by spearheading the landmine treaty, contributing to the establishment of the International Criminal Court, and signing the Kyoto Protocol, the first international agreement on climate change.

Canada's embrace of the extension of international law often puts us at odds with a superpower such as the United States because we cannot depend on sheer strength to achieve our goals. This is true on arms, it is true on rights, and it is true on trade. Our multilateralism is not the reflection of wishful thinking. It is the result of realism. We have to partner and collaborate with others to get much done.

When John Diefenbaker was elected, he used to fulminate about "the Pearsonalities" in the East Block, then the offices of the old Department of External Affairs. Ironically, Diefenbaker's minister of public works, Howard Green, came to get along famously with his civil servants and realized that a long war with the public service was thoroughly counterproductive.

Times have changed. The Reform Party's reverse takeover of the Progressive Conservative Party, and subsequent election as a minority government in 2006, meant that we have had a government that has never stopped acting as if it was in opposition. Foreign policy became highly centralized and ideologically controlled by the Prime Minister's Office. The same office dutifully kept a close eye on every memo. "Equity" became a bad word. "Responsibility to protect" and "human security" were forbidden, not to be spoken aloud because they were the products of the despised "liberal internationalism."

The phrase "international law" is now permitted, but "international humanitarian law" is not.

But the changes were more fundamental than the Orwellian correctness of the language police. Down with multilateralism, the United Nations, Africa, a balanced Middle East policy, China, Russia: the list goes on. It was a cocktail consisting of 50 percent ignorance and 50 percent ideological claptrap. Over time, the cocktail became more sophisticated, but it remains just as lethal.

What have been lost in all this are issues of great substance. Our military effort in Afghanistan was never matched by diplomatic imagination, not because our public servants in Ottawa, Kabul, Kandahar, Islamabad, Delhi, and other capitals didn't—and don't—have talent and dedication, but because the political leadership was missing. Mr. Harper finally discovered China and Asia, but only after years of lost time, effort, and opportunity. These advances have taken too long, and the country has paid a high price.

One area in which we continue to play entirely on the margins is the Israeli-Palestinian issue. The decision to turn the issue into a domestic play rather than an opportunity for serious diplomacy means that real influence and respect have been replaced by the soapbox. This approach is at odds with our history, our long-term self-interest, and the interests of all sides in the region.

Canada's support for the creation of the state of Israel in 1948 never meant we were indifferent to the plight of the

Palestinians or the importance of the wider Arab world. Indeed, our role in 1956 and 1967 at the United Nations was a signal that we have long understood the need for mutual recognition and peaceful coexistence in the Middle East. In a regional sense, Canada's past participation with U.N. peacekeeping efforts was a clear indication of our commitment to peace and mutual recognition, as was our chairmanship of the Refugee Working Group as part of the negotiating process for a lasting agreement between Israelis and Palestinians that began in earnest in the early 1990s.

Before Mr. Harper took office, every government, whether Liberal or Conservative, made a point of emphasizing the non-partisan nature of our response to the Arab-Israeli, and more particularly the Palestinian-Israeli, conflict. We are supporters of the formation of the state of Israel and of Israel's right to live in peace with its neighbours, with borders and boundaries that are internationally protected and recognized. The Palestinian aspiration to statehood cannot be denied. Its sovereignty side-by-side with the state of Israel will bring a better chance of long-term peace. The difficult issues between the parties on borders, boundaries, and refugees need to be negotiated within the framework of international law, with as much assistance from the outside world, including Canada, as will contribute to a positive and workable outcome.

If we see the region as a simple conflict between good and evil, where our job is nothing more complicated than to pick sides, we abandon the tradition of diplomacy, peacekeeping, and attempting to find solutions that has been at the heart of Canadian life since 1945. I have my own rule of thumb. Every country, indeed every family, is more complex and diverse than

official ideologies would have you believe. So the man of the
house who looks me straight in the eye when I'm canvassing
and solemnly pronounces that "this house" votes this way or
that is belied by the quiet smile or wink of a wife or child in-
dicating that Mr. All Pow-
erful doesn't really know
what he's talking about.

*If we see the region as a
simple conflict between
good and evil, where
our job is nothing more
complicated than to pick
sides, we abandon the
tradition of diplomacy,
peacekeeping, and
attempting to find
solutions that has been
at the heart of Canadian
life since 1945.*

And so it is with coun-
tries. My frequent trips to
the Middle East only reinforce the point. In Tel Aviv,
my wife, Arlene, and I once
toured a K–12 school for the
children of illegal immigrants
of one kind or another. A
steady stream of African refugees cross through Egypt
and the Sinai Peninsula and
arrive on Israel's doorstep.
They are not Jews. They
are seeking a refuge, a job, a
home. The official line is that
they are illegal and should be
deported. But their advocates want them to stay, and they remind
the country of its humanitarian traditions and obligations under
international law. In the meantime, the kids need schooling, and
Tel Aviv's progressive mayor decided to make it happen. The
school is open from 7:30 in the morning to 7:00 at night, gives the
kids three meals a day, and provides full education with music
and art programs.

Some Israelis complain of "the Republic of Tel Aviv," whose diversity and liberalism will lead to the end of the Jewish state. One secular cab driver I met said that the demands of religious Orthodox Jews for state support and special support "are more outrageous than the Palestinians." And so it goes. There are as many as fifty thousand "illegals" in Tel Aviv. The number could be higher and grows each day.

In 1948, many Palestinians fled Israel, and many of them still call the declaration of Israeli independence a day of disaster and mourning. In high school, I had an Egyptian math teacher, Mr. Nawar, who was from a Coptic family that had left Egypt when Nasser's coup unleashed an Arab nationalism that made the Nawar family feel unwelcome. The Suez Crisis made it worse. After 1948, Jews all over the Middle East were made to feel brutally unwelcome, and so they steadily left their homes, from Morocco to Iran, where they had lived for centuries. The Christian component of the Arab community, always a powerful presence, has been leaving in droves, the bombs in Alexandria and Baghdad only being the most recent example of the violence that majorities can inflict on "strangers" who have in fact as strong a claim on citizenship and birthright in the eastern Mediterranean as anyone else.

Religious prejudice combines with secular nationalism to create a brew that can be intoxicating and that has become lethal. When former Iranian president Mahmoud Ahmadinejad told a New York audience in 2007 that "we have no homosexuals in Iran," what he really meant was "when we find them, we kill them." This refusal to accept diversity and pluralism as the norm, and not the exception, is a terrible

plague around the world. Fighting it is one of the truly worthy causes of our time.

We should not make the mistake of thinking this is primarily a military struggle. It is about education. It is about values. It means more democracy, not less, more pluralism, not less, and refusing to let the preachers of intolerance and hatred have their way.

———

The toxic brew of prejudice and violence came powerfully to the world's attention with the bombing of the World Trade Center on September 11, 2001, but Canadians should have become more fully aware after the Air India massacre sixteen years before, on June 23, 1985. We chose to dismiss it from our minds as a tragedy that had to do with a conflict in a far-away country. In reality, the bomb was made in British Columbia, put on a plane in Vancouver, transferred to another plane in Toronto, and blown up off the coast of Ireland with 329 passengers on board, most of whom were Canadians. The masterminds and perpetrators of the atrocity were not jailed, with two of those charged found not guilty and only one behind bars for having helped build the bomb. Several reviews and a royal commission later, we are more aware of the fact that most everything that could have gone wrong did indeed do so, of the failures of the Royal Canadian Mounted Police and Canadian Security Intelligence Service to communicate properly, and of the deeper consequences of our collective denial as a country to embrace this event as a truly Canadian tragedy.

When one reads the reports written about the attacks on

the World Trade Center, it is hard to avoid the feeling that if we had learned important lessons earlier from Air India and shared those conclusions more emphatically with other countries around the world, that the tragedy in 1985 might not have been repeated in 2001. It is the same story—failures of imagination and intelligence, agencies more concerned with turf than results, and a refusal to accept the extent of the risks and dangers of the modern world.

As we deal with these issues in the aftermath of the more recent attacks in Ottawa and Quebec, in Paris and Europe, it is easy to see how the worst aspects of politics can take over in such situations. The temptation to use the crisis to reinforce other kinds of messaging takes over. "Stephen Harper wants to create a police state." "Tom Mulcair is soft on terrorism." "Justin Trudeau isn't up to the job." And on it goes.

The Air India bombing should have taught us, and all countries, that we are not immune from the violence of the world, that one certain consequence of our being in the world and the world being in us is that this doesn't just mean we are a multicultural and multiracial country. It means we are in the world, warts and all. That the warts indicate the reality, as well as the threat, of violence does not mean that borders can be forever closed or that the "war" with those who claim to be speaking for some twisted version of extremist Islam is one fought by arms alone.

We have to be vigilant in defence of our security, and we need the deepest and most efficient cooperation between our intelligence services, the RCMP, and local police forces. We do not yet have that, and it is a continuing, practical challenge. But Canada also has a Charter of Rights and Freedoms, and the

Constitution requires that we remain vigilant in defence of due process as much as we are in the defence of freedom.

As a country of immigrants, we are home to the world's great religious faiths. We need to do more to ensure that we are all talking to one another, that we do not allow differences to fester or extremism to grow. That requires a willingness to engage, cooperation between all levels of government, and one more thing: a willingness to name the problem itself.

President Obama's refusal to use the words "Islamic extremism" or anything that connects what is happening with the formation of the aspiring state known as the Islamic State of Iraq and the Levant (ISIL) to Islam strikes me as a bit precious. He quite rightly wants to make it clear that there is no war between Islam and the West and that practitioners of the Muslim faith are not the enemy. But it is wrong to ignore the theological pretensions of ISIL and its followers, and it is wrong not to realize that, given the organization's appeal to Muslim youth in the West, it will require the engaged leadership of the many different Islamic faiths and tendencies to win the battle.

If governing in the name of a theory is a bad idea, so is invading in the name of a theory.

The rules of the game have not changed. A century that gave us unprecedented violence has now been succeeded by a new world of bewildering complexity and brutality. Simplistic thinking has no place in it. If governing in the name of a theory is a bad idea, so is invading in the name of a theory. Avoiding ideological enthusiasm, doing less harm, ensuring more security and therefore saving more lives, reconciling differences, eliminating the worst poverty, steadily constructing a world order step-by-step based on the rule of law—all these are worthy goals. They are the way forward, for Canada, and for the world.

We are seeing emerge in our country something that works deeply against this need for engagement. It is a new isolationism that has its adherents on the right and the left. It is fuelled by the painful effects of the recession that make us all worry about the future and how a complicated world seems to be making our lives more difficult and less prosperous.

We are missing the opportunity to advance Canada's genuine interests and risk a deeper isolation than we have faced since the late 1930s.

This new isolationism is also fed by leaders who confuse spin with explanation or conflate command and control with creating a sense of vision and direction. We are not, today, even remotely leaders on any of the critical issues facing Canada and the world. The disengagement from diplomacy has had its comic moments, but now the consequences are far more serious. We are missing the opportunity to advance Canada's genuine interests and risk a deeper isolation than we have faced since the late 1930s. This does us no good. And we shall pay an even higher price as time goes on.

Conclusion

Samuel de Champlain came to Canada in the early seventeenth century formed by his experiences in a Europe literally torn apart by religious and ethnic conflict. The "great and good place" he saw in Canada was to be marked by a spirit of reconciliation and a recognition of the rights and traditions of all—Catholics, Protestants, nonbelievers, and the Aboriginal people he encountered as he travelled through eastern and central Canada.

The people and institutions he left behind did not always live up to his hopes and expectations. Violent conflict, death by disease and neglect, struggles between English and French—our early history was not often marked by civility.

But as the refugees flowed north from the United States after the Revolutionary War, and as immigration continued from Europe, a new vision began to take hold in the provinces of British North America. While the supporters of the Family Compact wanted a government that would insist more on order than on liberty, the irresistible arguments for freedom and for responsible government began to win out. Voices calling for responsibility, accountability, the separation of church and state, and a universal right to public education rose above those who simply preferred the status quo, or worse, who rioted against policies of social progress and change.

The country underwent a great transformation as a result of the turmoil caused by the industrial and democratic revolutions of the nineteenth century. The industrial revolution gave rise to a working class that could not accept the hardships and inequalities to which it was subjected, and so took to protest and politics as a necessary way of increasing their power and leverage. They demanded that governments start responding to their needs. A momentous change occurred, from economies and societies based on hierarchy and conformity to those composed of people who insisted that their voices be heard and that authority be made accountable and transparent.

At the same time, political thinkers grew dissatisfied with the lockstep marriage between ideas of freedom and laissez-faire economics. Practical political philosophy had to shift. If freedom meant the ability to do things, rather than simply the right to be left alone, then the state had to change, evolve, and become more active.

My vision of Canada begins with this history and pairs with it ideas about individual conscience, freedom, and dignity.

It is predicated on an understanding of economic freedom and the government's role in ensuring a strong capacity for regulation and the rule of law. How else do we make sure that personal liberty does not become a licence to abuse power? For each person to achieve his or her freedom, society needs to help break down the barriers to human potential. The power of this idea is felt today in societies around the world that fail to respect the rule of law, that disregard diversity, that believe that the power of the party or class or privilege is more important than the primacy of freedom.

I see a Canada that is determined to increase the franchise of its citizens and that is at the forefront of expanding the rights of people around the globe. It is a country able to see beyond a world divided by privilege, wealth, and colour to one determined by equal rights and the sense that a good country is one where people care about what happens to one another. It is a country whose politicians will embrace individuals' successes, the creation of wealth, and a never-ending effort to open up opportunities for its residents. Prosperity, innovation, social justice, and sustainability will be at the centre of every political debate.

But we're not there yet. When Laurier spoke of "Canada first, Canada last, Canada always," he was speaking to an emergent nationalism, to a country that wanted to be itself, not just an offshoot of empire. There are, even now, those who are happy if Canada becomes a willing follower of another empire. But most Canadians are not among them. They don't want their government to become a branch plant of the American Tea Party. They have proudly rejected saying "ready, aye, ready" to every American military adventure and every intellectual adventure that comes out of the right-wing movements in the United States.

Most Canadians want our country to chart its own course, not oblivious to world events or changing realities. What is required is an unprecedented effort of engagement, both at home and abroad. We need to learn to think and act consequentially, logically, and without illusions. We are our own worst enemies in this regard. Politics is about pursuing the common good. We can join together and build on our successes in providing common services, or we can see them eroded in a rush to imitate those societies that have allowed the ties of mutual support to become frayed to a point where they can't be recognized.

Most Canadians want our country to chart its own course, not oblivious to world events or changing realities.

This book has not been written as an exercise in partisan propaganda. My intention has been to show the resonance and resilience of a way of looking at politics that is based on assessments of values, ideas, programs, character, and leaders, not on spin, money, image, impressions, branding, and appeals to fear or even hate. It is important to understand the extent to which our political world has become much more about the latter than the former and that we are the poorer for it. Canada is not at all alone in living through this transformation, and we can see its effects in other countries as well as our own. Regardless of who wins an election, certain issues will persist in time and will have to be addressed. Ideologists of the right and left won't like that, but it's true. Politics is too important to be left to the politicians.

At a recent dinner where ideas and feelings about the political game were being shared, someone asked me if I had any personal regrets about having spent so much of my adult life in politics. My answer was a simple no. In fact, quite the contrary. I can imagine no life more full of personal challenge and emotional reward. It is not for the faint of heart, or the queasy in stomach, but it deserves our best efforts.

This book has not been written as an exercise in partisan propaganda. My intention has been to show the resonance and resilience of a way of looking at politics that is based on assessments of values, ideas, programs, character, and leaders, not on spin, money, image, impressions, branding, and appeals to fear or even hate.

Further Reading

In addition to the books I refer to in the text, here are a few recommendations that I hope will open some more doors.

I have written in my earlier books about my family, political experiences, and lessons learned. I contribute a regular column to the online edition of the *Globe and Mail*. I also have a website, www.bobrae.ca, as does my law firm, www.oktlaw.com.

One of the best recent books about European and Canadian politics in the 1930s and 1940s is David Halton's biography of his father Matt Halton, *Dispatches from the Front*. As you read it, it is worth reflecting on how journalism is the same, and also how it has changed.

Years ago I read Vance Packard's book about advertising, *The Hidden Persuaders*. It still resonates today. More recently I learned much from reading *Shopping for Votes* by Susan

Delacourt, as well as Paul Wells's blogs and his book about Stephen Harper. Gallup and Rae's *Pulse of Democracy* (Simon and Schuster 1940) is still an interesting read. Joseph Stiglitz's *The Price of Inequality* (Penguin 2012) is invaluable. Nate Silver's *The Signal and the Noise* (Penguin 2013) provides a necessary background to statistics and probability, and he is one of the few modest pollsters. Have a look at his website FiveThirtyEight.com for ongoing commentary that is always interesting. Sasha Issenberg's book *The Victory Lab* (Broadway 2012) is the single best analysis on big data and modern politics. George Lakoff's book *The Political Mind* explores the use of language in politics, and applies Orwell's insights in a compelling way. Alison Loat and the Samara Foundation continue to do important work in assessing the fate of our parlimentary democracy. Brent Rathgeber, who resigned from the Conservative caucus, has outlined his concerns about parlimentary democracy in his book *Irresponsible Government*.

There is a vast literature on leadership, as well as an endless array of websites and material on the web. Garry Wills's book is an excellent introduction to the challenge of political leadership and followership. Studies of political leaders are equally numerous. The late Martin Gilbert spent a lifetime studying Churchill, and he has written a one-volume biography. Roy Jenkins's book is readable. Arthur Herman's *Gandhi and Churchill* provides a fascinating perspective, as does the classic little study by Robert Rhodes James, *Churchill: A Study in Failure*. James MacGregor Burns's work on Roosevelt comes in two volumes. He also wrote a valuable book, *Leadership*. H. W. Brandes and Conrad Black have both written Roosevelt biographies worth reading. The best analysis of leadership and the gritty nature of the political process can be found in Robert Caro's masterful four volumes, so far, on the life of Lyndon Baines Johnson. No better political read can be found anywhere.

I have recommended Nelson Mandela's great book *The Long Walk to Freedom* before. I do so again.

On Macdonald, see Richard Gwyn's two-volume biography. There is no equivalent book about Laurier, although Andre Pratte's little study is very good. John English has written an outstanding biography of Pierre Elliott Trudeau, again in two volumes.

On the broad issue of why issues seem to have become more important, and why it's harder to discuss them, see Joseph Heath's book *Enlightenment 2.0*. David Foot's *Boom, Bust & Echo* made a lot of people more aware of the importance of demographics, and the author has a lively website for his company, Footwork Consulting. On health care, read both the Romanow and Kirby reports, Jeffrey Simpson's book *Chronic Condition*, and keep your eye on provincial budgets. Both the Criminal Code and the Income Tax Act are much thicker than they used to be. It's worth asking why that has to be the case.

There are several books that have helped illuminate the understanding of the issues facing indigenous people in Canada. Thomas King's *The Inconvenient Indian* is a brilliant survey, and so are John Ralston Saul's optimistic *A Fair Country* and *The Comeback*. For a completely different perspective, with which I disagree, Tom Flanagan has written *First Nations? Second Thoughts*, *Beyond the Indian Act*, and his two books on Louis Riel, *Louis "David" Riel* and *Riel and the Rebellion*.

Flanagan's most recent book, *Persona non Grata,* is a good description of what happens when you get thrown under the bus.

Out of the many books worth exploring, James Daschuk's *Clearing the Plains* has rightly won many awards and prizes. John Long's *Treaty No. 9* is a thorough analysis of what happened in 1905 and 1906 in the far north of Ontario. Mark Abley's *Conversations with a Dead Man* is an imaginative and provocative look at the life of Duncan Cameron Scott, Canadian poet and administrator of the Indian Act and residential schools. Both the Royal Commission on Aboriginal Peoples and the Commission on Truth and Reconciliation have produced massive amounts of material to move our souls. To this point, moving our will to action seems to be a different matter.

Acknowledgments

My family has supported me wonderfully in this as in all other projects. Arlene and I have discussed it in its various phases, and her insights have always made a difference. My daughters Judith, Lisa, and Eleanor have been key advisors even without knowing it.

My sister, Jennifer, and brother, John, as well as my sister-in-law, Ginny, have been a wonderful source of support this past year as in all others.

When I decided to retire from federal politics a second time, I was ably assisted in the transfer to civilian life. Jeremy Broadhurst, Kate Purchase, and Craig Knowles were, as always, gracious and thoughtful. My former assistant at the House of Commons, Danya Vered, helped me with a search of the archives and did it with her usual skill and good humour.

Acknowledgments

My colleagues at Olthuis Kleer Townshend LLP have been wonderfully hospitable to me in innumerable ways. I want in particular to thank John Olthuis, Renée Pelletier, Bryce Edwards, Andrea Bradley, Kaitlin Ritchie, Cathy Ball, and Stobo Sniderman, who have helped me with teaching and writing and much else besides.

I have also had the benefit of working closely with elected leaders, elders, and many fine advocates in Aboriginal communities across the country.

I am lucky to teach at the University of Toronto and am grateful to the then Director of the School of Public Policy and Governance, Mark Stabile, as well as my colleague and friend Mel Cappe. The Faculty of Law, its dean, Edward Iacobucci, and many faculty members have been equally welcoming. Above all I want to thank my students in "The Role of Government" and "Aboriginal Law and Policy" who have been unafraid to challenge my views and have helped me to think more clearly.

I write twice a month for the online edition of the *Globe and Mail*, thanks to an invitation from Natasha Hassan in 2013, shortly after I resigned from parliament. Douglas Saunders and Rob Gilroy have been consistently helpful. Some ideas that found their way into *Globe* Online columns have been further developed in these pages.

To recite the names of all those who have guided me in life and politics would take a full book in itself. But I hope all fully realise how deeply grateful I am for the insights, good humour, and deep support I have been lucky enough to receive from many people across the country and indeed around the world. One person in particular I would like to thank is Jonathan

Goldbloom, who led the team in the 2006 leadership bid and has continued to be a valued friend and advisor.

Kevin Hanson, Phyllis Bruce, and Brendan May of Simon & Schuster and their wonderful production and editing teams have goaded, inspired, prodded, and above all helped me write and finish this little book in near record time. I am deeply grateful to them for all their efforts.

The dedication to this book is to my parents, Saul and Lois. Without them I would not be here, and neither would the modest arguments in this book.

Index

Abley, Mark, 144
Aboriginal peoples, 75–93, 102,
    120–21, 143–44
  colonialism and, 76, 78–81
  Constitution on, 36, 75, 89
  crisis of governance in, 77–78
  environmental policy and,
    59, 60
  incarceration rate in, 77, 100,
    101
  population growth in, 75, 76,
    93
  pre-contact civilization of, 78
  public opinion on, 93
  residential schools for, 77, 81,
    86
  self-government negotiations
    with, 89, 113
  treaties and (*see* Treaties)

Afghanistan, 40, 126
Africa, 124
Ahmadinejad, Mahmoud, 129
Air India massacre, 130–31
Alberta, 5, 59, 81, 83, 89, 90
Apartheid, 124
Apprenticeships, 61
Aral Sea, 62
Asia, 52, 126
Attawapiskat, 77
Austerity measures, 54
Australia, 11

Baby boomers, 11, 50–51
Baghot, Walter, 107
Beccaria, Cesare, 99
Bégin, Monique, 68
Bell Canada, 72
Bennett, Richard, 60

Bentham, Jeremy, 99
Beothuk, 78
Berle, Adolf A., Jr., 30
Beyond the Indian Act
    (Flanagan), 143
Bismarck, Otto von, 50
Bison, extinction of, 85
Black, Conrad, 142
Bloc Québécois, 46
Bobrae.ca, 141
Boom, Bust & Echo (Foot), 143
Borden, Robert, 60, 121
Bouchard, Lucien, 39
Bourassa government, 38
Brains Trust, 30
Brandes, H. W., 142
Brazeau, Patrick, 45
Brennan Center for Justice,
    100–101
Bring Up the Bodies (Mantel), 17
British Columbia, 59, 81, 82
British Institute of Public
    Opinion, 27
Broadbent, Ed, 35, 36, 46
Brundtland Report, 63
Burke, Edmund, 24
Burns, James MacGregor, 26,
    142

Calder v. British Columbia,
    82–83, 91
Cameron, Malcolm, 85

Camp, Dalton, 37
Campbell, Kim, 49
Canada Health Act, 68–69
Canada Pension Plan, 3
Canadian Pacific Railway, 18,
    84–85
Canadian Security Intelligence
    Service, 130
Capitalism, 61–63
Carbon pricing, 59, 60
Caro, Robert, 143
Census, long-form, 15–16
Centennial celebration, 3–4
*Certain Trumpets: The Nature of
    Leadership* (Wills), 24
Chamberlain, Neville, 27–28
Champlain, Samuel de, 135
Charlottetown Accord, 89, 111,
    113–14
Charter of Rights and Freedoms,
    33, 35–37, 98, 102–3, 131
Cherokee Nation, 92
China, 6, 58, 126
Chippewas, 76
Choctaws, 92
Chrétien, Jean, xii, 35, 114–15
    election funding laws and,
        20–21
    health care policy and, 69
    leadership skills of, 42–43
    refusal to support Iraq
        invasion, 124–25

Index

Chronic Condition (Simpson), 143

Churchill: A Study in Failure (James), 28, 142

Churchill, Winston, 27, 28–29, 35, 123, 142

Clark, Joe, 34

Clearing the Plains (Daschuk), 144

Clinton, Hillary Rodham, 39

Colonialism, 76, 78–81

Comeback, The (Saul), 143

Communist economies, 62

Compulsory voting, 10–11

"Concept of Public Opinion and Its Measurement, The" (Rae), xi

Conservatives, 105–6, 127
    Aboriginal peoples and, 84
    criminal justice system and, 100, 101
    economic policy and, 54
    leadership of, 43
    message management and, 14–15
    voter turnout and, 10, 13

Constitution, 33, 102, 132
    on Aboriginal peoples, 36, 75, 89
    patriation of, 35–37, 97
    on the Senate, 111–13

Conversations with a Dead Man, 144

Coughlin, Charles, 27

Criminal Code, 100, 143

Criminal justice system, 16, 99–103
    incarceration rates in, 77, 100, 101, 103
    opposing philosophies of, 99–100

Daschuk, James, 85, 144

Davis, Bill, 36, 37, 104

Delacourt, Susan, 141–42

Delgamuukw case, 83

Democracy, 95–116
    constitutional, 93, 95–97
    criminal justice system and, 99–103
    federalism and, 97–99
    government-citizen connection and, 113–16
    individual rights and, 98–99

Democracy (*cont.*)
    Parliament and, 102, 103–10
    populist (majoritarian), 93, 96–97, 103
    the Senate and, 110–13

Demographics, 50–52, 101

Diefenbaker, John, 35, 38, 60, 124, 125

Dion, Stéphane, 44–45, 59

Dispatches from the Front (Halton), 141

Douglas, Tommy, 35, 46, 80
Durkheim, Emile, 70

Economy
collapse of, 4–6
crisis of 2008-09, 5–6, 9, 52,
53–54, 115
growth in, 5, 53–55, 56
inequalities in, 3, 56
policy on, 52–57
recovery of, 43
Education, 3, 50, 51, 54, 56, 64
Elections. *See* Voting/elections
"Electoral symbolism," 21
Employment, 3
Ending House Arrest for
Property and Other
Serious Crimes by Serious
and Violent Offenders Act,
68
Energy sources, 59–61
English, John, 143
Enlightenment 2.0 (Heath), 143
Environmental policy, 51, 57–63
capitalism and, 61–63
specific recommendations for,
59–61
Established Programs Financing
Act, 68
Eugenics, 80
Euro, 115
Europe, 54, 58
European Union, 53

External Affairs Department,
123, 125
"Extinction clause" in Williams
Treaties, 76

Fairclough, Ellen, 35
Fair Country, A (Saul), 143
Fairweather, Gordon, 35
Family Compact, 136
Federal budget, 4, 6, 43, 52, 68
Federalism, 97–99
Fireside Chats (Roosevelt),
29–30
First Casualty, The (study),
17–18
First Nations, 72, 75, 77, 79, 81,
83–84, 89, 90, 92, 101
First Nations? Second Thoughts
(Flanagan), 143
FiveThirtyEight.com, 100, 142
"Fix it for a generation" plan, 66
Flaherty, Jim, 52
Flanagan, Tom, 88, 143–44
Foot, David, 143
Ford, Henry, 25
Foreign policy, 117–33
Israeli-Palestinian issue and,
126–29
new isolationism in, 133
prime minister's office control
of, 125
proposed approach to, 118–20
Suez Crisis and, 122–24, 129

Index

Forsey, Eugene, 105
Fossil fuel subsidies, 59
France, 79, 122
French Revolution, 7, 24

Gallup, George, xi, 142
Gallup polls, 12
Gandhi, Mohandas, 28
Gandhi and Churchill
    (Herman), 142
George III, King of England, 79
Germany, 61, 95
Gilbert, Martin, 142
Ginsberg, Morris, xi
Givens, Phil, 44
Goods and Services Tax, 44
Great Britain
    Aboriginal peoples and, 79
    Canadian foreign policy and,
      121
    Parliament of, 107, 108–9
    Suez Crisis and, 122
Great Depression, 4, 27, 29, 121
Greece, 53
Green, Howard, 125
Gregg, Allan, 15
Gwyn, Richard, 143

Hall, Emmett, 82
Halton, David, 141
Halton, Matt, 141
Harper, Stephen, 13, 14, 43, 60,
    68, 107–8, 126, 127, 131, 142

economic policy and, 52
electoral laws challenged by,
    20, 21
health care policy and, 66
Kelowna Accord and, 77
leadership skills of, 44–45, 46
Senate reform promised by,
    111
Harris, Mike, 68
Health care, 3, 50, 51, 65–72
    extra billing practice in, 68–69
    hospitalization, 65, 68
    medication access and, 56, 69
    mental health, 66, 69–72
    partisanship impact on, 67–68
Heath, Joseph, 143
Hébert, Chantal, 114
Herman, Arthur, 142
Hidden Persuaders, The
    (Packard), 141
Hitchens, Christopher, 15
Hitler, Adolf, 27, 28, 122
Holmes, Oliver Wendell, 31, 55
Hoover, Herbert, 30
House of Commons, 71, 105,
    106, 107, 108, 110, 113
Human rights, 91–92, 121
Humphrey, John, 122

Ignatieff, Michael, 44–45
Immigration, 51, 128–29, 135–36
Incarceration rates, 77, 100, 101,
    103

Index

Income Tax Act, 100, 143
Inconvenient Indian, The
    (King), 143
India, 58, 124
Indian Act, 76, 77, 80, 91
Industrial revolution, 136
Infrastructure, 51, 54, 60
Innu Nation, 90
International Criminal Court,
    125
International law, 125, 126, 127
International Monetary Fund, 53
Inuit people, 70, 92, 121
Iran, 41, 129–30
Iraq, 40, 124–25
Irresponsible Government
    (Rathgeber), 142
Islam, 131–32
Islamic State of Iraq and the
    Levant (ISIL), 132
Israel
    entrepreneurial culture of,
        64–65
    Palestinian conflict and,
        126–29
    Suez Crisis and, 122
Issenberg, Sasha, 7, 8, 10, 142

Jackson, Andrew, 92
James, Robert Rhodes, 28, 142
James Bay Agreements, 60
Jenkins, Roy, 142

John, King of England, 96
Johnson, Lyndon Baines, 143

Kelowna Accord, 76–77
Keynes, John Maynard, 30
King, Mackenzie, 34
King, Thomas, 143
Kipling, Rudyard, 53
Kirby Report, 69, 143
Klein, Naomi, 61
Korean conflict, 123
Kyoto Protocol, 125

Labrador, 90
Lakoff, George, 142
Landmine treaty, 125
Lapierre, Jean, 114
Laski, Harold, xi, 30
Laskin, Bora, 35, 82
Laurier, Wilfrid, 18, 32–33, 34,
    137, 143
Layton, Jack, 46
Leadership, 23–47
    confluence of events and,
        24–25, 26, 39
    defined, 23
    historical examples of, 26–31
    implementation and, 23–25,
        46
    persuasion and, 23–25, 46
    public opinion and, 27–29,
        40–41

Index

the self and, 26, 31
successful transitions of, 43
vision and, 23–25, 29, 31,
 36–37, 39, 40, 46
Leadership (Burns), 142
League of Nations, 121
Lewis, David, 35
Liberals, 104–6, 127
 health care policy and, 66
 leadership of, 34, 35, 42, 43,
 45–46
Loat, Alison, 142
Long, Huey, 27
Long, John, 144
Long Walk to Freedom, The
 (Mandela), 143
Louis "David" Riel (Flanagan),
 143

Macdonald, John A., 18, 32–33,
 34, 60, 84, 143
Macmillan, Harold, 25–26, 124
Magna Carta, 96
Malinowski, Bronislaw, xi
Mandela, Nelson, 124, 143
Manitoba, 81, 83, 89, 90
Manning, Preston, 38–39
Mantel, Hilary, 17
Marie Antoinette, 7
Marshall, John, 92
Martin, Paul, 43, 69, 76
McCain, John, 40

McGinniss, Joe, 19
McKenna, Frank, 38
McLachlin, Beverley, 102–3
Media, 19, 50, 73, 109
Medicare, 50, 52, 106
Meech Lake Accord, 38, 113
Megaphone diplomacy, 118
Mental health, 66, 69–72
Mental Health Commission, 72
Métis people, 92
Miller, Frank, 105
Mississaugas, 76
Moley, Raymond, 30
Montreal exposition, 4
Morning After, The (Hébert and
 Lapierre), 114
Moynihan, Daniel Patrick,
 117–18
Mulcair, Tom, 46, 131
Mulroney, Brian, 37–39, 60, 124
Municipalities, 98
Mussolini, Benito, 27

Nasser, Gamal, 129
National Citizens Coalition, 20
NATO, 122
Natural resources, 57–58
Nawar, Mr. (author's math
 teacher), 129
New Deal, 30–31
New Democratic Party (NDP),
 13, 35, 36, 46, 104–6

Nigeria, 53

1984 (Orwell), 15

Niqab, discussion over, 97

Nixon, Richard, 42

Nobel Peace Prize, 122

Northwest Territories, 82

Nunavut, 82

Obama, Barack, 7–8, 14, 39–41, 132

Obamacare, 66–67

Oil, 5, 52, 53, 57, 60

Oktlaw.com, 141

Omnibus bills, 109

Ontario, 4, 50, 81, 83, 86, 89, 90

Orwell, George, 15, 142

Orwellian language, 15, 68, 126

Ottawa, 131

Packard, Vance, 141

Palestinian-Israeli issue, 126–29

Parizeau, Jacques, 97–98

Parliament, 9, 36, 102, 103–10.
  See also House of
  Commons; Senate
  British, 107, 108–9
  dysfunction and polarization
    in, 50
  elections and, 103–5, 107
  minority, 104–6
  omnibus bills in, 109
  partisanship in, 108

Pawley government, 38

Pearson, Lester B. ("Mike"), 34, 122–23, 124

Persona non Grata (Flanagan), 144

Peterson, David, 69, 105

Policy, 49–74
  demographics and, 50–52
  economic, 52–57
  environmental, 51, 57–63
  foreign, 117–33
  health care, 50, 51, 65–72

Political Mind, The (Lakoff), 142

Political picnics, 18

Politics, 1–22
  advertising in, 18–19
  business model of, 8–10
  discarding of truth in, 16,
    17–18
  dismissal of reason in, 16
  the economy and, 4–6
  message management in,
    14–15
  permanent campaigns in, 7,
    14, 22
  polls and, 12–13
  propaganda in, 17–19
  spending in, 18–21

Polls, 12–13

Population
  Aboriginal, 75, 76, 93
  of Canada, 93

Prairies, 81, 84, 85

Pratte, Andre, 143
"Precarious workers," 6
Price of Inequality, The
  (Stiglitz), 142
Prime minister (office of), 103,
  107–8, 109, 112, 125
Progressive Conservative Party,
  35, 125
Pulse of Democracy, The (Gallup
  and Rae), xi, 142

Quebec, 3, 46, 59, 82, 111,
  113–15, 131
Quebec Act, 79
Quebec Round, 38
Question Period, 9, 14, 73, 108
Quiet Revolution, 3

Racism, 77, 78, 80, 100
Rae, Arlene Perly, 69, 128
Rae, John, xii
Rae, Lois, x, xi
Rae, Saul, x–xi, 23, 117–18, 142
Railway construction, 81,
  84–85
Rathgeber, Brent, 142
Reagan, Ronald, 44
Reform Party, 43, 111, 125
Refugee Working Group, 127
Retirement age, 50, 109
Riel, Louis, 143
Riel and the Rebellion
  (Flanagan), 143

Roeder, Oliver, 100–101
Romanow Commission report,
  69, 143
Romney, Mitt, 40
Roosevelt, Franklin, 26–27,
  29–31, 40, 142–43
Roosevelt, Theodore, 31, 42
Royal Canadian Mounted Police
  (RCMP), 130, 131
Royal Commission on
  Aboriginal Peoples, 76,
  144
Royal Proclamation of 1763,
  79
Rule of justice, 95–96
Rule of law, 95–96, 97, 102, 103,
  125, 137
Russia, 6, 53, 62

Samara Foundation, 142
Saskatchewan, 68, 81, 83, 84, 89,
  90
Saul, John Ralston, 143
Scott, Duncan Campbell, 86, 87,
  144
Scott, Frank, 35
Selling of the President, The
  (McGinniss), 19
Seminoles, 92
Senate, 110–13
September 11 attacks, 130–31
Shopping for Votes (Delacourt),
  141–42

Signal and the Noise, The (Silver), 142
Silver, Nate, 142
Simpson, Jeffrey, 143
Sinclair, Murray, 92
Social Darwinism, 80
Socialism, 61–63
Social media, 7
South Africa, 124
Spence, Wishart, 82
Spencer, Herbert, 80
St. Laurent, Louis, 123
Stalin, Josef, 27
Stiglitz, Joseph, 142
Suez Crisis, 122–24, 129
Suicide, 69–71, 91, 102
Supreme Court of Canada, 36, 97, 98, 110, 111–12
 on Aboriginal rights, 82–83, 85, 88, 102
 on criminal justice system, 102–3
 on political spending, 19
Supreme Court of the United States, 19, 92
Sustainable development. *See* Environmental policy

Taxes, 4, 44, 55, 56, 64
Tea Party, 55, 137
Terra nullius concept, 79
Terrorism, 40–41, 130–32

This Changes Everything (Klein), 61
Thomas, Norman, 30
Three *p*'s of parliamentary politics, 73
Thunderchild, Chief, 85
Tories, 104
Trade, 4, 38, 58, 120
Trail of Tears, 92
Transportation, 3, 50
Treaties
 coerced signing of, 84–86
 Constitution on, 36
 differing narratives on meaning of, 86–87
 historic, 81–90
 land covered by, 82–83
 modern, 81, 83, 90
 need for renewal and updating of, 90
 oral terms ignored in, 88
 Williams, 76
Treaty 6, 84–86, 88
Treaty 9, 84, 86–87
Treaty No. 9 (Long), 144
Treaty of Paris, 79
Triple E Senate, 111
Trudeau, Justin, 45–46, 131
Trudeau, Pierre, 33–37, 68, 104, 143
Truth and Reconciliation Commission, 92, 144

Index

Tsilhqot'in case, 83
Tugwell, Rexford, 30
Turner, John, 37, 42, 43

Unemployment, 4, 54
United Nations, 63, 117–18,
    122–24, 127
United Nations Emergency
    Force (UNEF), 122, 124
United States, 80, 107, 135
    Canada's differences with,
        125, 137–38
    financial crisis (2008-09) in,
        8, 54
    incarceration rate in, 101
    Native Americans of, 92
    Obamacare in, 66–67
    political spending in, 19
    recent elections in, 7–8
    September 11 attacks in, 130–31
    trade with, 4, 120
Universal Declaration of Human
    Rights, 122

Venezuela, 53
*Victory Lab, The: The Secret
    Science of Winning*

Campaigns (Issenberg), 7,
    10, 142
Voting/elections, 7–14
    "creating the electorate" in,
        7
    declining participation in,
        10–11, 13–14
    parliamentary, 103–5, 107
    segmentation of the electorate
        in, 8–9

"Wait care guarantee," 66
Wannsee conference, 95
Webb, Beatrice, xi
Webb, Sidney, xi
Wells, Clyde, 38
Wells, Paul, 142
Williams Treaties, 76
Wills, Garry, 24, 142
World War I, 17, 121, 123
World War II, 27–28, 122,
    123
Wynne, Kathleen, 59

Younger generation, 10–11,
    13–14, 51
Yukon, 82